REALITY AND RHETORIC

REALITY AND RHETORIC
Studies in the Economics of Development

P. T. Bauer

Harvard University Press
Cambridge, Massachusetts
1984

Library of Congress Cataloging in Publication Data

Bauer, P. T.
    Reality and rhetoric

    Includes index.
    1. Economic development.   2. Developing countries –
Economic conditions.   3. Economic assistance – Developing
countries.   I. Title.
HD82.B333   1984   338.9   83–18389
ISBN 0–674–74946–4

Contents

Preface

In the preparation of this book I have worked even more closely with Professor B. S. Yamey than in my other writings. He is co-author of Chapters 3, 6, 7 and 8, both of their earlier versions and their present form. But he has also been closely involved in all the studies published here, from their inception to the current printed version. As indicated in Chapter 1, the frequent use of the plural pronoun is intended to refer to joint argument and joint work.

Once again I have benefited considerably from the editorial assistance of Léonie Glen. Her quick understanding, intelligent drafting, good nature and remarkable working capacity have left their mark throughout the book.

I should like to thank Dr Brian Hindley and Dr Deepak Lal for thoughtful suggestions for the improvement of an earlier draft of Chapter 2.

I wish to thank Miss Mary de Vere Chamberlain, my secretary, who has typed most of this book, some of it several times over and often in trying conditions, but always in good temper and good humour.

Some of the material has been published before, but in practically every case this version has been much extended and revised. The status in respect of the various studies is as follows.

Chapter 1 has not been published before. It is a revised form of the first lecture in the World Bank's Pioneer Lectures delivered at the Bank in February 1982. It will be incorporated eventually in a World Bank publication of this lecture series. Each of six economists was asked to lecture on what he considered to be his contribution to the study of development economics; hence the somewhat auto-biographical nature of the chapter.

Chapter 2 is a substantially revised version of an essay prepared for the Trade Policy Research Centre, to be included in a forthcoming volume by the Centre under the title *Global Strategy for Growth*.

Chapter 3 is a much enlarged version of a short essay which first appeared in *The Public Interest* (New York), Summer issue, 1982.

Chapter 4 is a much amended version of a paper presented at a conference in memory of the late Wilson E. Schmidt, held in Washington DC in March 1983.

Chapter 5 is a greatly extended and revised version of a paper presented at a conference organized by the American Enterprise Institute for Public Policy Research in Washington DC in July 1981. A much abridged and unrevised version of the conference paper appeared in *This World*, New York, Vol. 1, December 1981.

Chapter 6 was first published in *Encounter*, in the course of 1983.

The original version of Chapter 7 was published in the *Economic History Review*, second series, Vol. XXV, No. 4, November 1972.

Chapter 8 first appeared in the *South African Journal of Economics*, Vol. 22, No. 2, June 1954.

Chapter 9 first appeared in the *Journal of Development Economics*, Vol. 2, 1975. It was a reply, requested by the Journal's editor, to a review article of an earlier book of mine. In this chapter, therefore, I have limited myself to minor stylistic changes. I have, however, omitted two sections and occasional passages that directly overlap with material included in other chapters in this book.

Chapter 10 has not been published before.

In conclusion, I may conveniently note here some matters of terminology. Unless stated otherwise, references to the war are to the Second World War; the terms underdeveloped world, less developed world, less developed countries (ldcs), developing world or countries, the Third World and the South are used as synonyms (these terms are examined critically in Chapter 3); and aid refers to official government-to-government economic aid, and thus excludes military aid, commercial investment and the work of voluntary agencies.

London, August 1983

CHAPTER 1

Remembrance of Studies Past: Retracing First Steps

1

The following is a reasonable summary of the principal components of the burgeoning development literature of the early post-war years.

External trade is at best ineffective for the economic advance of less developed countries (ldcs), and more often it is damaging. Instead, the advance of ldcs depends on ample supplies of capital to provide for infrastructure, for the rapid growth of manufacturing industry, and for the modernization of their economies and societies. The capital required cannot be generated in the ldcs themselves because of the inflexible and inexorable constraint of low incomes (the vicious circle of poverty and stagnation), reinforced by the international demonstration effect and by the lack of privately profitable investment opportunities in poor countries with their inherently limited local markets. General backwardness, economic unresponsiveness and lack of enterprise are well-nigh universal within the less developed world. Therefore, if significant economic advance is to be achieved, governments have an indispensable as well as a comprehensive role in carrying through the critical and large-scale changes necessary to break down the formidable obstacles to, and initiate and sustain the process of, growth.

These ideas became the core of the mainstream academic development literature, which in turn has served as the basis for national and international policies ever since. Even when some elements of the core have disappeared from more academic writings, they have continued to dominate political and public discourse, an instance of the lingering effects of discarded ideas.

My earliest investigations of economic issues in ldcs were not inspired by these topics, in fact they were altogether unconnected with them.[1] I came to this general area through two studies, one of the rubber industry of South-East Asia and the other of the organization of trade in the former British West Africa. I spent more

1

than ten years on these studies during the 1940s and fifties, when I was for substantial periods in each of the two regions. What I saw was starkly at variance with the components of the emerging consensus of mainstream development economics listed above. My enquiries into and observation of economic, social and political life in these two major regions provoked a lasting interest in general development economics. Although my ideas have developed much since the completion of these studies, they have not moved closer either to the tenets of the development orthodoxy of the 1950s or to their subsequent modification.[2]

2

Even before setting foot in South-East Asia and West Africa I knew that their economies had advanced rapidly (even though they were colonies!). After all, it required no instruction in development economics to know that before 1885 there was not a single rubber tree in Malaya nor a single cocoa tree in British West Africa. By the 1930s rubber, cocoa and other export crops were being produced on millions of acres, the bulk of them owned and cultivated by non-Europeans. But while I knew this and a good deal else about local conditions, I was nevertheless surprised by much of what I saw, including the extensive economic transformation of large areas and the vigour of economic life of much of the local populations. In Malaya (now Malaysia), for example, the economic activity of the many towns and large villages, the excellent communications and the evident prosperity of large sections of the non-European population reflected a world totally different from the largely empty and economically backward Malaya of the nineteenth century. The results of somewhat similar though less extensive changes were evident also in West Africa, most notably in Southern Nigeria and the Gold Coast (now Ghana). How was all this possible if there was any real substance in the central ideas of the contemporary development economics?

In the earliest stages local supplies of capital were minimal. However, in South-East Asia the export market for rubber (and to a lesser extent other products such as tin) attracted investment by European enterprises, particularly for such purposes as the development of rubber estates in hitherto empty jungle. Where local labour supplies were inadequate, as in Malaya and Sumatra, the Western enterprises organized and financed large-scale recruitment and migration of unlettered workers, mainly from China and India. The activities of the Western enterprises induced unintended and unexpected sequences. For instance, Chinese traders were drawn into the rubber trade. Some started their own plantations while others brought seeds and consumer goods to the indigenous people of Malaya and Netherlands India (now Indonesia). They thereby encouraged the local population to plant rubber trees and to produce for the market. By the late 1930s, over one-half of the rubber acreage of South-East Asia was owned by Asians. This acreage represented the results of capital formation through direct investment in the face of initially low incomes.[3]

The history was somewhat different in West Africa. In this region there were (and are) no European-owned plantations. The large area under cocoa, groundnuts, cotton and kola nuts has been entirely on farms established, owned and operated by Africans. The extensive capital involved was made available partly by European trading firms which financed local traders, and partly by direct investment by Africans, the latter in important instances carried out by migrant farmers in regions far from their homes. In all this the role of traders was crucial. Sir Keith Hancock has rightly called West Africa 'The Traders' Frontier'. The traders made available consumer goods and production inputs, and provided outlets for the cash crops. Their activities stimulated investment and production. The part played by what used to be called inducement goods – a term once a household expression but rarely encountered in modern development literature – was notable. The sequence showed the inappropriateness of the notion of the 'international demonstration effect', the idea that access to cheap consumer goods, especially imported goods, retards development in the ldcs by raising the propensity to consume of the local populations.

The rapid economic progress generally, of which the large-scale capital formation in agriculture by the local people was a major component, cannot be squared with the idea of the vicious circle of poverty and stagnation. It would have been a freak of chance if I had happened on the only two regions in the less developed world whose

3

peoples had managed to escape the imperatives of a law of economics. In fact, of course, the notion of the vicious circle of poverty, that poverty is self-perpetuating, is belied by evidence throughout the developed and less developed world, and indeed by the very existence of developed countries.

The notion is not rescued by the suggestion, much canvassed since the 1950s, that the production of commodities for export resulted merely in enclaves operated by Westerners without benefit to the local people. As I have said, a large part of production and sometimes the entire output was (and remains) in the hands of the local population. The same applies to the associated activities of trade and transport. Had this been otherwise, the development of export crops could not have transformed the lives of the local people as it had done. In these regions, as in many others, pervasive economic advance has made it possible for much larger populations to live longer and at much higher standards.

A developed infrastructure was not a precondition for the emergence of the major cash crops of South-East Asia and West Africa. As has often also been the case elsewhere, the facilities known as infrastructure were developed in the course of the expansion of the economy. It is unhistorical to envisage an elaborate and expensive infrastructure as a necessary groundwork for economic advance. And countless people in trading and transport often performed the services usually associated with capital-intensive infrastructure. For instance, human and animal transport, contacts between numerous traders, and long chains of intermediaries were partial but effective substitutes for expensive roads and communication systems.

3

The historical experience I have noted (which had its counterpart in many ldcs) was not the result of conscription of people or the forced mobilization of their resources. Nor was it the result of forcible modernization of attitudes and behaviour, nor of large-scale state-sponsored industrialization; nor of any other form of big push. And it was not brought about by the achievement of political independence; or by the inculcation in the minds of the local people of the notion of national identity: or by the stirring-up of mass enthusiasm for the

4

abstract notion of economic development; or by any other form of political or cultural revolution. It was not the result of conscious efforts at nation building (as if people were lifeless bricks, to be moved about by some master builder), nor of the adoption by governments of economic development as a formal policy goal or commitment. What happened was in very large measure the result of the individual voluntary responses of millions of people to emerging or expanding opportunities created largely by external contacts and brought to their notice in a variety of ways, primarily through the operation of the market. These developments were made possible by firm but limited government, without large expenditures of public funds and without the receipt of large external subventions.

The nature of these responses in turn exposed for me the hollowness of various standard stereotypes. It was thus evident that the ordinary people of the ldcs were not necessarily torpid, rigidly constrained by custom and habit, economically timid, inherently myopic or generally deficient in enterprise. In the space of a decade or two, the illiterate peasantry of South-East Asia and West Africa planted millions of acres to produce new cash crops; and rubber, cocoa and kola trees, for example, take five years to become productive. In all, this represented large volumes of direct investment made possible by voluntary changes in the conduct, attitudes and motivations of numerous individuals, in many cases involving the sacrifice of leisure and the modification of personal relationships. Yet Malays, Indonesians and Africans were precisely among those who were depicted (as they still sometimes are) as incapable either of taking a long view or of creating capital, and as being hobbled by custom and habit.

The establishment and operation of properties producing cash crops are entrepreneurial activities. So also are the ubiquitous trading and transport activities of local people. The contention is thus invalid that in ldcs entrepreneurial skills and attitudes are lacking. Indeed, they are often present but take forms which accord with people's attributes and inclinations, and with local conditions and opportunities.

In many parts of the less developed world there is evidence of much enterprise and risk-taking, often on a small scale individually, but by no means confined to agriculture and trading. It is not necessary to spell out details here.

The contribution to economic development of the numerous small- and large-scale entrepreneurs (farmers, traders, industrialists and so on) highlights the generally melancholy record of the entrepreneurial efforts of ldc governments, all too often financed at large cost from revenues derived from the taxation of the producers of cash crops. It is often urged in the development literature, in support of the alleged need for extensive state control and direction in the economies of many ldcs, that their populations lack entrepreneurial talents. However, should the people of a particular country in fact be without entrepreneurial talents or inclinations, it is difficult to see how the politicians and civil servants from this population could make up for the deficiency.

In the less developed world, willingness to bestir oneself and to take risks in the process is not confined to entrepreneurs in the accepted sense of the term. Hundreds of thousands of extremely poor landless rural people have migrated thousands of miles to improve their lot. The large-scale migration from South-East China and South India to Fiji, Malaya and Netherlands India is well known. In my work I was able to show that very poor illiterate people were well informed about economic conditions in distant and alien countries, and that they responded intelligently to the opportunities they perceived.

4

When I began my work, the emerging ideas on economic development assigned decisive importance to the ratio between numbers of people on the one hand, and available resources, that is land and other natural resources as well as capital, on the other. Given the size of population, physical resources were all. Apart from age and sex differences, people were envisaged as homogeneous from an economic point of view. All this can be seen in the construction of the growth models of contemporary economic literature, and in the more general discussion these inspired. The only partial qualification was provided in the growing emphasis on human differences resulting from capital embodied in people.

My existing scepticism about this approach was soon and amply reinforced by what I saw in South-East Asia. The differences in economic performance and hence in achievement among groups were immediately evident, indeed startling. Perhaps the clearest demonstration that people, even with the same level of education, cannot be treated as uniform in the economic context was to be found in that region.

Many rubber estates kept records of the daily output of each tapper, and distinguished between the output of Chinese and Indian workers. The output of the Chinese was usually more than double that of the Indians, with all of them using the same simple equipment of tapping knife, latex cup and latex bucket. There were similar or even wider differences between Chinese, Indian and Malay small-holders when I visited several hundred smallholdings in Malaya in 1946. The pronounced differences between Chinese and Indians could not be attributed to the special characteristics often possessed by migrants, as both groups were recent immigrants. The great majority of both Indians and Chinese were uneducated coolies, so that the differences in their performance could not be explained in terms of differences in human capital formation. The Chinese performance in Malaya was especially notable. Not only had practically all the Chinese been very poor immigrants, but they were also subject to extensive adverse discrimination imposed by the British administration and by the local Malay rulers.

Of course, differences among groups were not limited to rubber tapping or to other aspects of rubber production. They were pervasive throughout the local economies in the establishment and running of plantations and mines, and of industrial and commercial undertakings. These differences in no way resulted from differences in initial capital endowments of the differential groups. In fact, of course, these differences meant that the various groups made vastly different contributions to capital formation; and these contributions in turn were conditioned not only by differences in productivity but also by differences in personal preferences, motivations and social arrangements. I was to encounter similar phenomena in West Africa, in the Levant, in India and elsewhere.

I should not have been so greatly surprised by what I found. After all, I was aware of the pronounced differences in economic perform-ance among different cultural groups as a feature of much of

7

economic history, and of the fact that groups discriminated against were often especially productive and successful. My temporary oversight was probably due to my having succumbed to the then prevailing view that the less developed world, newly discovered by Western economists, was somehow different. I had also fallen victim to the notion of the primary and overwhelming importance of physical resources (including capital) as determinants of real incomes, a short period of aberration in which I had ignored what I knew of economic history. And I, like others, may have been bemused by figures of average incomes calculated for entire populations without regard to ethnic (or for that matter age) composition.

I might note here that many millions of very poor people in the Third World today, as in the past, have ready access to cultivable land, and that conventional labour-to-land ratios are meaningless. Such groups as aborigines, pygmies and various African tribes are extreme cases of poverty amidst abundant land. Even in India, much land is officially classified as uncultivated but usable.

The small size and low productivity of so many farms in the Third World primarily reflect want of ambition, energy and skill, and not want of land and capital. In any case, it was borne in on me that the notion of uncultivable land is misleading, since cultivability depends heavily upon the economic qualities of the people as well as on official policies affecting the use of land. Examples of the last point include the price policies of governments, control of immigration and inflow of capital, and the terms on which state lands are made available.[4]

In all, although their discussion has been largely taboo in the post-war development literature, the reality and importance of group differences in economic performance cannot be disputed. The subject is virtually proscribed in the profession, even when these differences serve as major planks in official policy, as they do in Malaysia and elsewhere.

Discussion of the reasons for group differences in performance and of their likely persistence would be speculative, and economic reasoning is not informative on these questions. But this provides no excuse for the systematic neglect of group differences by economists. Such differences are plainly relevant for assessment of the economic situation and prospects in Third World countries (and elsewhere too), and for the concept and implications of population pressure. It

8

follows also that the relation between economic development and population growth cannot be examined sensibly on the basis simply of numbers and resources.

5

Considerations such as those set out so far have reinforced my reluctance to attempt to formulate a theory of economic development, and also my rejection of theories based either on sequential stages of history or on the conventional type of growth model. The inadequacy of these theories is in any case revealed by their inability to account for the well-attested phenomenon of economic decline (whether absolute or relative decline). Moreover, economic development is but one facet of the history of a society, and attempts to formulate general theories of history have so far been conspicuously unsuccessful, even though many distinguished minds have been addressed to the question. Not surprisingly, some of these attempts have yielded informative insights, but none of sufficient generality to serve as basis for a theory of development.

In the more narrowly economic context, I found the approach embodied in the conventional growth models to be unhelpful and even misleading. The approach focuses on independent variables which I came to know were unimportant. Again, it ignores the interplay between the chosen variables and parameters. Thus the models take as given such decisive factors as the political situation, people's attitudes and the state of knowledge.[5] Attempts to increase the stock of capital, for instance by special taxation or restriction of imports, greatly affect these and other factors treated as parameters, and these repercussions typically far outweigh the effects on development of any increase in capital which might ensue. These shortcomings are apart from basic problems of the concept and measurement of capital, and of the distinction between investment and consumption. This distinction is especially nebulous in the conditions of ldcs where the use of inducement goods often results in improved economic performance, and consumption is thus complementary to rather than competitive with saving and investment.

Since the Second World War an aggregative and quantitative approach has predominated in development economics. Such an approach may have been inspired by the growth models which confine themselves to aggregates such as capital, labour and consumption. Acceptance of this general approach has had the comforting corollary that the economy of an ldc could be studied on the basis of readily accessible statistics; and also that it was legitimate to dispense both with direct observation and also with non-quantitative information generally. This neglect in turn has led to an uncritical acceptance of the available statistics. The very large biases in international income statistics, as well as changes in their incidence over time, have been ignored in much of development economics. Again, in the statistics used in development economics, direct capital formation in agriculture has been under-valued, or more often neglected altogether. Yet this form of capital formation is quantitatively and qualitatively significant in the advance from the largely subsistence activities characteristic of many ldcs.

Perhaps more serious in its repercussions has been the failure to recognize this form of capital formation in analyses of economic growth, and hence in proposals for promoting growth. Thus fiscal policies for accelerating capital formation have often been advanced without recognition of their necessary effects on direct capital formation in agriculture. In practice, the untoward results of this oversight have been compounded by the habit, itself encouraged by the aggregative approach, of the neglect of prices as determinants of the choice of economic activities.

The use of occupational statistics presents some instructive examples of inappropriate reliance on accessible statistics and of the neglect, even atrophy, of direct observation. Occupational statistics suggested that in ldcs almost the entire population was engaged in agriculture. For instance, this was a theme of the official reports on West Africa and the literature based on them which I consulted before my first visit. Trade and transport barely figured in the official censuses, or in Lord Hailey's *An African Survey*. I was therefore much surprised by the volume of trading activity and the large numbers of traders that I was soon able to observe. It became clear that the official statistics were misleading because they did not and could not reflect the prevailing incomplete occupational specialization. In households classified as agricultural it was usual for some of the members to trade regularly or intermittently, regardless of sex and also largely regardless of age.

West African experience, which was clearly not unique except perhaps in the extent of participation in trading, led me to examine and overturn the prevailing Clark-Fisher hypothesis that economic advancement entails a movement of labour progressively from primary to secondary and then to tertiary economic activity. I showed that the theory rested on misleading statistics; that tertiary activities were a miscellany of activities united only by their output being non-material; that they did not have the common feature of high income elasticities of demand, and that many tertiary activities were indeed necessary for emergence from subsistence production in poor countries; that in small-scale trade and transport in ldcs, labour can easily be substituted for capital; and that the belief was unfounded that technical progress was necessarily more pronounced in the production of goods than in that of services. Furthermore, the common aggregation of economic activities into three distinctive groups was shown to be of no value for analysis or for sensible policy prescriptions. Yet the notion is still alive and well that the tripartite classification of economic activities is not only valid and firm but can serve as basis for policy.

In the general context of development economics, the various preceding examples of misleading aggregation are overshadowed by a practice which I have not yet discussed here. This is the treatment of the world as being two distinct aggregates, the rich and progressing countries and the poor and stagnating countries. The second and much larger aggregate consists of practically the whole of Asia and Africa and the whole of Latin America. This collectivity is envisaged as broadly uniform, caught in a vicious circle of poverty, and separated from the former aggregate by a wide and widening gap in incomes, and afflicted moreover by generally deteriorating terms of trade in its exchanges with that other aggregate.

In fact, this picture does not bear any resemblance to reality. It does not do justice to the rich variety of humanity and experience in the less developed world, and to the rapid growth of many poor countries and the prosperity of large groups there. The inappropriate lumping together of all so-called ldcs has made it more difficult for economists and others to reject the prevailing notions to which I have drawn attention at the beginning of this chapter, and therefore to

11

recognize the inappropriateness of the policy prescriptions derived from them. I now see far more clearly than I did when my studies began how inappropriate was the division of the world into the two supposedly distinct aggregates.

6

In the early post-war development literature trading activity was very largely ignored. It was ignored in the statistics, in the discussion of development prospects, and in the planning literature as well as in the plans themselves. When considered at all, the discussion of trade was couched typically in pejorative terms. For instance, it was viewed as a hotbed of imperfections and as a source or manifestation of waste. Hence there followed policy proposals for the replacement of private trading arrangements by the establishment of state trading and state-sponsored co-operative societies.

In contrast, the indispensable role of traders, especially in the development of cash crops, was evident in my enquiries both in South-East Asia and in West Africa, and in other ldcs I came to know.

I noted what had often been observed by economic historians, administrators and other observers, that traders provided and extended markets and thereby widened the opportunities open to people as producers and consumers.[6] Traders brought new and cheaper goods to the notice and within the reach of people, a process which served as inducement to improved economic performance. Sometimes small-scale traders penetrated areas before explorers and administrators had reached them. Without trading activities there could be no agricultural surplus. Traders linked producers and consumers, served to create new wants, and encouraged or even made possible the production necessary for their satisfaction. More generally, they acquainted people with the workings of an exchange economy and the attitudes appropriate to it. By extending people's economic horizons and by establishing new contacts, the activities of traders encouraged people to question existing habits and mores, and promoted the uncoerced erosion of attitudes and customs uncongenial to material progress. Moreover, trading widely proved to be a seedbed of entrepreneurial activities extending beyond trading

12

itself. Thus enterprising and successful traders at times initiated or expanded their farming interests (many in any case were part-time farmers). Trading brought to the fore entrepreneurs who perceived economic opportunities and were ready to pursue them. It was not surprising that successful transport and manufacturing enterprises were often established by traders, both local and expatriate.

These dynamic effects of the activities of traders were largely ignored in the post-war development literature. The role of traders in bringing about a more effective inter-regional and inter-temporal allocation of output may have been more widely recognized. But even where this was recognized, the activities of traders and the organization of the trading system were subjected to much misconceived analysis and criticism. For example, the multiplicity of traders and the vertical sub-division of trading activity into many successive stages were often criticized. I showed that these features could be explained in terms of the relative scarcity of capital and administrative skills, of substitution possibilities in trade of labour for capital, and of the availability of large numbers of people for part-time or full-time trading activity. My observations and analysis of trading activities and arrangements gave rise to much subsequent work by economists and anthropologists. Professor Walter Elkan has gone as far as to suggest that this early work pioneered recognition of the presence and significance of what has come to be termed the informal sector in less developed countries, and initiated the study of its economics.[7]

Further, my work enabled me to expose the underlying flaws in familiar proposals and policies for restructuring the trading sector in ldcs. These measures ranged from restriction of the numbers of traders and the enforced elimination of particular stages in the chain of distribution, to large-scale state support for co-operative trading, and to the suppression of private traders and their replacement by state trading organizations. The adoption of such measures in various ldcs has had the unsurprising consequences of restricting the opportunities for producers and consumers, of entrenching inefficiency in the trading sector, and of obstructing economic progress and the widening of horizons.[8] Most of these so-called reforms have caused widespread hardship and have also locked many people into subsistence production.[9]

7

Since at least the 1930s, both popular and academic literature has
decried the fluctuations in the prices of primary products, especially
those produced in ldcs. Commodity stabilization schemes have now
been major items on the agenda for several decades.

Commodity schemes have usually been proposed as instruments
for the reduction of price fluctuations. In practice, however, the
objective has usually been the monopolistic raising of prices. This is
transparent today when commodity schemes are envisaged as a form
of resource transfer from the West to the Third World. But the
monopolistic intention was clear already in inter-war regulation
schemes such as the International Rubber Regulation Scheme. I was
to study this in detail, and was able to document that while rubber
regulation did not stabilize prices, it did widen fluctuations in output
and probably also in producer incomes. Among other untoward
effects, it imposed hardship on potential producers who were
generally much poorer than were the beneficiaries.

Subsequently I examined in depth the operations of the official
West African Marketing Boards. These state organizations were
given the sole right to buy for export and to export the controlled
products. (In technical language, they had monopsony powers of
purchase.) The proclaimed purpose of these arrangements was to
stabilize the prices received by producers and even to improve them.
In fact, they promptly developed into a system of paying producers
far less than the market value of their produce – they were, in effect,
an instrument of heavy, persistent and discriminatory taxation. And
over extended periods they destabilized producer prices and
incomes. I drew attention to major effects of this heavy taxation,
notably that it reduced the development of cash crops and of private
savings, obstructed the emergence of a prosperous African peasantry
and middle class, and served as a dominant source of money and
patronage for those with political power. Thus, paradoxically, while
stabilization is typically invoked as cover for monopolistic raising of
producer prices, in this instance it was invoked as cover for persistent
under-payment of producers made possible by the monopsony
powers of the boards.[10]

My work on rubber regulation and on the marketing boards had various spin-offs. First, it showed that the smoothing of fluctuations needs to be distinguished clearly from other objectives of official schemes such as monopolistic raising of prices, or taxation of producers by under-paying them. Second, it also showed that even if the reduction of fluctuations was the genuine objective of a scheme, its implementation would run up against formidable conceptual and practical problems. These included the problems of maintaining contact with the long-term trend of prices; of choosing between the setting of producer prices at the discretion of the authorities and their setting in accordance with an announced formula; of choosing between stabilization of prices and stabilization of producer incomes; and of choosing the frequency and amplitude of the adjustments in producer prices. Third, my work, and the response it elicited from Professor Milton Friedman,[11] led me to question whether the exercise of government power was desirable or necessary for producers to achieve price or income stabilization if they felt the need for it. If stabilization of disposable incomes is desired, producers on their own account can set aside reserves on which to draw in times of adversity. If necessary, they can form voluntary associations to help them achieve this purpose.

8

The truth of the French saying *rien ne vit que par le détail* impressed itself upon me in the course of my work in South-East Asia and West Africa. Much of this work uncovered phenomena and relationships which had not been acknowledged adequately either in previous studies of these regions, or in the more general economic texts. I list briefly a number of these matters not already discussed in this chapter; fuller treatments are to be found elsewhere in my publications. However, several of the issues raised or illustrated are of some general significance and interest.

The supply of smallholders' rubber had commonly been instanced as a classic case of a backward-sloping supply function. In fact, it was possible to establish not only that the supply curve was forward-rising, but also that this was fully recognized in the implementation of official policy (as, for instance, in the imposition of special export taxes to curtail smallholders' exports under rubber regulation). The much higher density of planting on rubber smallholdings than on the estates used to be attributed to the crude methods used by smallholders. In fact, it could be shown to reflect differences in the availability of factors of production to the two broad groups of producers. Further, even the short period supply price of rubber could not be estimated simply by reference to current outlays, but had also to include the expected reduction of future revenues through the current consumption of the latex-containing bark. Again, cost of production was found to vary greatly with the current product price (much more so than with the scale of operations). Thus cost of production, and therefore the supply price, depended significantly on expected future prices as well as on current prices. When it is recognized that current and prospective product prices affect costs, it is then not legitimate to treat supply as independent of demand (as is the standard practice in micro-economic theory).

I found that the standard expositions of monopoly and of its measurement were incomplete, even misleading. Rubber regulation covered many thousands of producers, none of whom controlled even two per cent of total supplies of a highly standardized product, or had any influence on prices. The controlling authority, on the other hand, faced a much less than perfectly elastic demand. This combination was very different from the situation typically analysed in monopoly theory. In the study of West African trade, statistics accessible to me showed that the degree of concentration was systematically higher for standardized products than for differentiated products. This was contrary to what I expected to find from contemporary discussions of product differentiation.

In both South-East Asia and West Africa, the number of trading points diminished steadily from the urban centres to the outlying rural areas. Yet I found this to have no systematic relation to the intensity of competition: the effective degree of monopoly could not be predicted at all reliably from the number of traders present. The small trader in a remote village was exposed to competition from many sources, including itinerant pedlars and farmers acting as part-time traders. However, the number of traders became important in determining the strength of competition whenever entry was officially restricted. Even then, diversity among the traders (such as

16

ethnic diversity or differences in length of establishment) could modify the effect of numbers on competition.

That detailed statistics can be revealing was shown by statistics of the prices of official rights to export rubber from Malaya. These could be made to reveal both the *de facto* extent of restriction, and the very low supply price of large quantities of smallholders' rubber. Close examination of the statistics of total estate production and those of locally registered companies disclosed the more favourable treatment under rubber regulation of United Kingdom registered companies than of locally registered companies, as well as of estates compared to smallholdings. The statistics could be used also to measure the effect of the one hundred per cent excess profits tax on the level of production.

Direct observation in conjunction with certain statistical series, especially transport statistics, helped to uncover the large volume and importance of kola nut production and trade in Nigeria, activities entirely in the hands of Africans and virtually unremarked in official and other publications. Again, detailed examination of the working of import and price controls in wartime and post-war West Africa made clear that quite momentous political and social consequences could follow from apparently innocuous official measures.

9

It was during the latter part of the 1950s that I first wrote on two major issues in development economics, namely comprehensive planning and foreign aid. I was subsequently to develop my analysis and conclusions when these two subjects came to loom more largely both in the academic development literature and even more in public discussion. I noted then that comprehensive central planning was certainly not necessary for economic advance and was much more likely to retard it. It did not augment resources but only diverted them from other public and private uses. It reinforced the authoritarian tradition prevailing in many ldcs, and it also divorced output from consumer demand and restricted people's range of choice.

On foreign aid I wrote little, beyond saying that it was not indispensable for the progress of poor countries and that it often served to underwrite and prolong extremely damaging policies commonly pursued in the name of comprehensive planning.

I see no reason to retract the findings and assessments set out in this summarized version of my earlier writings. But I must acknowledge a serious misjudgement. I failed then to appreciate the pervasive significance of the politicization of economic life in ldcs. Except in my treatment of the West African Marketing Boards, I was apt to analyse the more specifically economic implications and effects of individual policy measures without appreciating adequately how they contributed to the general politicization of life in many ldcs. By the late 1950s the principal measures included state monopoly of major branches of industry and trade, including agricultural exports; official restrictive licensing of industrial and other activities; controls over imports, exports and foreign exchange; and the establishment of many state-owned and state-operated enterprises including state-supported and state-operated so-called co-operatives. Several of these individual measures gave governments close control over the livelihood of their subjects. When applied simultaneously, these measures conferred even greater powers on the rulers.

In these conditions the acquisition and exercise of political power became all-important. The stakes, both gains and losses, in the struggle for political power increased. These developments enhanced uncertainty, anxiety and political tension, especially in the many ldcs which comprised distinct ethnic, religious or linguistic groups. They thereby diverted people's energies and resources from economic activity to the political arena.

These developments and their repercussions have become much more pronounced and widespread since the 1950s. Not only the economic but even the physical survival of large numbers of people have come to depend on political and administrative decisions. Productive ethnic minorities have been conspicuous among the victims. What I saw only dimly in the 1950s has therefore become a major theme in some of my more recent writings.

CHAPTER 2

Market Order and State Planning in Economic Development

1

Since the Second World War, it has been a major axiom of the mainstream development literature that comprehensive central planning is indispensable for the progress of poor countries. A further theme has been that commercial contacts between the West and less developed countries do not promote the development of the latter or even obstruct it, as for instance by interfering with the planning process.

These ideas are behind some of the major policies proposed in the literature. In this chapter I shall confront these ideas with evidence, mostly readily available evidence, from many parts of the less developed world.

In recent years, these opinions have become so widely accepted that their supporters no longer find it necessary to state them explicitly.[1] This is especially so with the insistence on development planning. Moreover, recent criticism of the market is often expressed in convoluted language, or in technical jargon supported by mathematical notation. It is therefore convenient to quote some Early Fathers whose influence is still pervasive.

2

I shall quote first and at some length the view of Professor Gunnar Myrdal, Nobel Laureate and one of the most influential contemporary social scientists. He said in 1956 in a widely publicized lecture:

> Now, what amounts to a sort of super planning *has* to be staged by underdeveloped countries with weak political and administrative apparatuses and a largely illiterate and apathetic citizenry. But *the alternative to making the heroic attempt is continued acquiescence in economic and cultural stagnation or regression which is politically impossible in the world today*; and this is, of course, the explanation why grand-scale national planning is at present the goal in underdeveloped countries all over the

19

globe and why this policy line is unanimously endorsed by governments and experts in the advanced countries.[2]

Elsewhere he wrote:

The special advisers to underdeveloped countries who have taken the time and trouble to acquaint themselves with the problem, no matter who they are . . . all recommend central planning as the first condition of progress.[3]

Professor Myrdal here ignored obvious general considerations as well as simple historical evidence. Some ldcs had been advancing rapidly, without planning, at the time he wrote. He begged the question as to how 'apathetic citizenry' would be galvanized into economic productivity by central planning and direction and, indeed, why they should be forced to change their attitudes and their ways. And it is now evident that it is not 'politically impossible' for ldcs to stagnate, or even retrogress, for such reasons as government policies or prevailing attitudes.

Professor Myrdal's general position on the indispensability of planning was not idiosyncratic. In 1964, the International Economic Association organized a Round Table in Tokyo on the subject of Economic Development in East Asia. One of the presented papers was by Professor H. Kitamura of Tokyo University, a prominent Japanese development economist who was then on the staff of the United Nations Commission for Asia and the Far East. He wrote:

Only planned economic development can hope to achieve a rate of growth that is politically acceptable and capable of commanding popular enthusiasm and support.[4]

This categorical statement had already been contradicted by the experience of Japan, and of many other Far Eastern countries including Hong Kong, Malaysia, the Philippines, Singapore, South Korea and Taiwan. But not one of the participants, all leading development economists from many different countries, commented on the evident incongruity between these facts and Professor Kitamura's statement. And I suspect that similar attitudes and reactions would be dominant at any re-run today of the Tokyo meeting of 1964.

Central planning can be interpreted in a number of different ways. The standard interpretation in the development literature is extensive state control of economic activity outside subsistence farming.

20

Comprehensive planning in this sense played no part in the development of the West or of Japan, nor in the progress of the many less developed countries which advanced rapidly in the hundred years or so before the Second World War. This is not surprising. Comprehensive planning does not augment resources. The resources used by planners have been diverted from other productive public or private uses.

The declared aim of comprehensive planning is to raise living standards. But its advocates do not explain how the controls they envisage promote this aim. They simply regard the case as self-evident. At the same time they often insist, as did Professor Myrdal in the lecture from which I have already quoted, that the policy requires the utmost general austerity, without resolving the obvious contradiction.[5]

Why should the overriding of private decisions increase the flow of income? The divorce of output from consumer demand by itself involves a reduction of general living standards. Moreover, it retards the process of economic development. The prospects of higher and more varied consumption usually serve to promote improved economic performance in poor countries, by encouraging people to move from subsistence production to production for the market, for instance.

The modish idea that commercial contacts with the West are unhelpful or even damaging to the economic prospects of less developed countries serves as specious rationalization for the restriction of these contacts. The idea that they are harmful has even led to proposals for large-scale severance of commercial ties between the less developed world and the West in the name of the collective self-reliance of developing countries (sometimes termed the delinking of these countries from international trade).[6] Such ideas are often welcomed by Third World rulers because extensive restriction of the external commercial contacts of their citizens often serves their own interests.

In fact, commercial contacts with the West have been the prime instruments of material progress in the Third World. In Asia, Africa and Latin America the level of material achievement declines as one moves away from the impact of Western contacts. To say that commercial contacts inhibit economic advance is the opposite of the

21

truth. This also reflects contempt for ordinary people by suggesting that they do not know what they are doing when they buy imports from the West, or produce for export to the West.

Here is an early formulation of Western evil-doing, a formulation which is both succinct and comprehensive. It comes moreover from a highly regarded source. The late Paul A. Baran was full Professor of Economics at Stanford from 1951 until his death in 1964, and an academic of international reputation, especially in development economics. Here is a passage from *The Political Economy of Growth*, Baran's principal publication on development, a book still widely read:

> To the dead weight of stagnation characteristic of pre-industrial society was added the entire restrictive impact of monopoly capitalism. The economic surplus appropriated in lavish amounts by monopolistic concerns in backward countries is not employed for productive purposes. It is neither plowed back into their own enterprise, nor does it serve to develop others.[7]

This statement is patently untrue. In the less developed world large industries such as the oil, copper, tin, rubber and coffee industries, to mention but a few, have been financed through reinvested profits.

3

The anomalous, even perverse character of the opinions quoted in the preceding section becomes even more evident when we look more closely at what economic development is about, and at the operation of the policies pursued in the name of economic planning.

Extension of the range of choice of people as consumers and producers is perhaps the most satisfactory criterion of economic development. In the words of Sir Arthur Lewis, 'the advantage of economic growth is not that wealth increases happiness, but that it increases the range of human choice'.[8]

Extension of the range of choice is most likely to be promoted by an economic order in which firms and individuals largely determine what is produced and consumed, where they will work, how much they will save and how they will invest their savings.

Societies are made up of very large numbers of people. Their constituent persons and families perceive better than do others, or are even the only ones who can perceive, their own circumstances, attitudes, preferences, opportunities and prospects. They are also best qualified to judge their own likely responses to changes in these conditions. In the aggregate, they also possess a vast amount of other pertinent knowledge which the signals and mechanisms of the market order transmit and diffuse. Such transmission and diffusion of knowledge is indispensable for social, economic, scientific and technical innovation.

No centralized agency, however powerful, can perform these functions effectively, not even by coercion. Attempts to perform them by coercion go counter, moreover, to the widening of people's choice, the basic criterion of economic development.

The advent of the computer with its phenomenal efficiency in processing quantifiable information has not affected these realities of economic life. There is no way of feeding into a computer either people's perceptions of their own preferences, faculties, opportunities and prospects, or their likely reaction to changes in them or the information and knowledge dispersed among the people who make up society.

The market order contrasts with a centrally-planned economy, in which government decisions largely direct people's economic conduct. It differs also from custom-dominated economies, in which people's economic activities are largely prescribed by custom. In reality, all economies are to some extent mixed. People's economic activities are always affected by government action, by custom, and by market conditions. The differences, however, are sufficiently pronounced to justify distinguishing between market-orientated economies, centrally-planned economies, and custom-dominated economies. Contemporary economic and political discussion is preoccupied largely with centrally-planned and market economies. This is why I deal here only with these two types of economic organization.

4

The recent history of the Third World provides many examples of developments that could not have been predicted on the basis of surveys of resources, or by forecasting techniques, or by assembling, somehow or other, available data at some central point.

23

Consider the rise and spread of the plantation rubber industry of South-East Asia. The rubber tree is indigenous to South America. There was not a single rubber tree in Asia until, in the late nineteenth century, rubber seeds were brought from Brazil, first to the Royal Botanical Gardens at Kew, and thence to Ceylon and Singapore. The soils of the rubber-producing areas are poor, but the rubber tree makes few demands on the soil. At that time there were only meagre local labour forces in South-East Asia, and plantation rubber is a very labour-intensive activity. But it was possible to attract many hundreds of thousands of workers from India and China. There was little local capital, but enterprising trading companies found capital in the West to finance the opening-up and equipping of estates, and to recruit managers and workers to operate these properties. The activities of these trading companies were soon followed by those of Chinese traders who brought rubber seeds and consumer goods to thousands of smallholders, and this enabled and encouraged the rural population to plant rubber. Most of these activities and responses took place in regions far away from the ports (not to speak of the distance from the main rubber-using countries) and were made possible by the establishment and extension of public security.

These processes interacted with developments elsewhere, such as the rapid growth of the motor industry in the United States, the rise of the oil industry, and the use of carbon black in the manufacture of tyres. Within a decade or two of the establishment of the first rubber plantation in South-East Asia, millions of acres were planted, both by Western-owned companies and by Asian smallholders. The hundreds of thousands (eventually millions) of estate labourers and smallholders did not know the end use of the rubber they produced. Nor did they have to know. They simply took advantage of the opportunities for improving their lot, which came to them as a result of complex processes which originated far away, and the outcome of which was transmitted to them by the market. All they needed to understand was the extension of their opportunities.

Between the 1880s and the 1920s, a large cocoa industry emerged in the Gold Coast (now Ghana) and Nigeria. The cocoa holdings were planted, owned and operated by Africans, who again did not know, and did not need to know, what cocoa was used for (at one stage many believed that it served as a fuel in the West). They simply found it worthwhile to plant the cocoa trees. The establishment of public security and the activities of merchants were indispensable for such unexpected developments in this inhospitable region.[9]

As noted in the preceding chapter, the readiness of the local populations of South-East Asia and West Africa to establish commercial crops which do not produce until five years after planting refutes the familiar stereotype about the inability or unwillingness of these people to look ahead in economic matters.

Computers could not have helped economists or other forecasters to predict these sequences, let alone to assemble and co-ordinate the diverse resources which went into the rise of the rubber and cocoa industries. Again, who could have predicted that Hong Kong, an empty rock in 1840, would evolve first into a substantial port, and then into a large trading centre and thereafter into a major industrial power? Teams of development economists and forecasters could not have collected or processed the information which the market system has supplied and which has elicited a rate of material progress far greater and more pervasive than that of the People's Republic of China, or that of the dirigiste economies of South-East and South Asia, regions with far more natural resources than Hong Kong.

5

The significance of the differences or contrasts between central planning and the market order extends far beyond economic life. In a freely operating market system people can decide where they work, what they buy, how much they spend or save and where they invest. For most people freedom of choice in these matters is crucial.

The market order minimizes the power of individuals and groups forcibly to restrict the choices of other people. Forcible restriction of the choice of others is what coercion means. Possession of wealth does not by itself confer such power on the rich. Indeed, in modern market economies the rich, especially the very rich, usually owe their prosperity to activities which have widened the choices of their fellow men, including those of the poor. Obvious examples are the fortunes made in mass production and mass retailing.

Critics of the market often dispute the reality and significance of the freedoms and choices protected by decentralized decisions, on

25

the ground that such choices are of little value to many people, notably the poor. This criticism is epitomized in the familiar jibes that the Ritz is open to all, or that the poor are free to starve. It is a criticism which is radically misconceived. The ability to use their resources to their own best advantage, in particular to choose their employment freely and to have different employers competing for their services, is especially important to the poor and to people of humble status. It is well-to-do and established politicians, academics, media men, clerics, writers and artists who are apt to dismiss economic choice as unimportant.

In the Third World, as in the West, the extension of opportunities presented by the market has been and is of critical significance for the poor. For instance, the production of cash crops has enabled very large numbers of people to emerge from the extreme poverty and insecurity of subsistence production. This process has often been accompanied by an extension of people's extremely restricted cultural horizons.

Again, the rise of the plantation and mining industries in South and South-East Asia has enabled hundreds of thousands of extremely poor, low-caste or casteless rural labourers from the interior of Madras to go to Malaya and Ceylon to improve their lot, and for equally large numbers of Chinese labourers to escape from the harsh economic, social and political conditions in South-East China. Plainly, poverty is not the same as unfreedom in the sense of being subject to coercion by others. This basic difference used to be recognized in the linguistic distinction drawn between poverty, serfdom and slavery.

In centrally-controlled economies there are wide inequalities of power between rulers and subjects. This is most evident in communist and socialist countries. There are also wide differences in income. The coercive power of the rulers aggravates the lot of the poorest and impairs their prospects of improvement. The unsatisfactory general economic performance of socialist or communist economies also impairs the living standards of the poor.[10]

The choices promoted and protected by the market system transcend economic life. Decentralized economic decision-making is closely related to other components of personal freedom, including expression of opinion, and movement of people and their property. It is not accidental that these elements of freedom are to be found in market societies, not in closely controlled economies. Contrast conditions in the United States and the Soviet Union, the Federal Republic of Germany and the German Democratic Republic, Hong Kong and the People's Republic of China. In a fully socialized economy, the state owns the means of production, including those of production and distribution of information. It is therefore ultimately the only employer. In closely controlled economies, even when they are not completely socialized, people are not allowed to export capital, and their right to leave is also often restricted. Altogether, a market order is a necessary condition of personal freedom. It is not a sufficient condition, although in practice its operation tends also to erode other restrictions on this freedom.

I may mention in passing that the difference in political effectiveness between rulers and their subjects is generally much wider in the Third World than in the West. This is particularly so in much of Asia and Africa. The rulers in contemporary Asia and Africa tend to be drawn from the urban population; they are most likely to be people such as professional politicians, Westernized intellectuals or politicized members of the military. These groups have great power over the inarticulate rural population, and little sympathy for it. This discrepancy in effectiveness is reflected in the way economic controls are operated.

In closely controlled economies, the decisions of politicians and civil servants take the place of private decisions in production and consumption. Economic life is extensively politicized. Official directives replace voluntary transactions. The decisions of the rulers largely determine people's incomes and employment opportunities. Indeed, these decisions often determine the economic or even the physical survival of large sections of the population. In such conditions, who has the government becomes all-important for large numbers of people. Familiar examples from the recent history of the Third World include the fate of the Chinese in much of South-East Asia, of Indians in Burma, and of Asians in East and Central Africa. The attention, energies and resources of many people are then diverted from productive economic activity to the political arena, whether from choice or necessity; and this diversion of people's activities necessarily affects not only their own personal fortunes, but

27

the economic performance and progress of the whole society as well.

Thus, far-reaching politicization of life intensifies the struggle for political power, at any rate until all opposition is forcibly suppressed. Such conflict is particularly likely in heterogeneous countries. In many less developed countries, especially in Asia and Africa, different ethnic, tribal and cultural groups who had lived together peaceably for decades, even centuries, have been set against each other by the extensive politicization which has taken place since the Second World War. Evident examples include South-East Asia, Burma, Sri Lanka, East Africa and Nigeria. Clearly, the history of the Third World since the Second World War, and especially the extent and intensity of conflict, cannot be understood without acknowledgement or realization of this politicization, which is promoted by state economic control.

6

Criticism of central planning or of the policies pursued in its name must not obscure the importance of the essential tasks of government. The adequate performance of these tasks is indeed helpful to the effective operation of the market, if not necessary for it. The tasks include the successful conduct of external affairs, notably the defence of the country, and also the preservation and encouragement of external commercial contacts; the maintenance of public security; the effective administration of the monetary and fiscal system; the promotion of a suitable institutional framework for the activities of individuals; and the provision of basic health and education services and of basic communications.

Supporters of the market order may disagree legitimately on the appropriate range of these functions. But the adequate performance even of the barest minimum of these tasks would fully stretch the human, administrative and financial resources of the great majority of Third World governments. And many of these governments neglect even the most elementary of these functions while attempting close control of their country's economy, or even occasionally, while contemplating the coercive transformation of society. They often seem anxious to plan but are unable to govern. For instance, many Third World governments who operate, or try to operate, close economic controls are unable to maintain public security. Particular examples in recent years have included Burma, India, Indonesia, Nigeria and Uganda.

Some commonly encountered criticisms of the market system ignore the simple fact that market participants are people. Human beings and their arrangements cannot be faultless. It is therefore not surprising that objectionable phenomena are to be found in the market order, including the operation of pressure groups, the contrivance of scarcities, attempts at coercion, and well-authenticated instances of fraud. But even when they are numerous, such phenomena do not serve as a valid basis for replacing the market by a controlled economy. In recent years, detractors of the market order have made much of instances of political pressure, or of fraud by market participants. Would it make for a better society if more people with such habits were in the government sector and thus possessed the coercive power which goes with it?

The market system should not be criticized because it cannot ensure material progress. Even governments which do not attempt central planning frequently pursue particular policies to inhibit economic advance, for instance by discriminating against productive groups. Again, for perfectly good reasons, many people may be unable or unwilling to change their established ways, or may be reluctant to take advantage of emerging economic opportunities. But such attitudes have nothing to do with the market system. In fact, market arrangements and peaceful external commercial contacts are more likely to bring about voluntary erosion of attitudes and customs uncongenial to economic improvement than are central direction and control. It is not a defect of the market that it does not guarantee material progress, let alone contentment or happiness. It is a corollary of voluntary arrangements that they permit people to remain materially unambitious or to consider the cost of economic improvement excessive if that is what they wish. The market order permits them to do their own thing, to use contemporary jargon.

The preceding arguments of this section are largely unrelated to the familiar criticism in the economic literature that the market process does not produce the optimum allocation of resources as defined in formal economic theory. Much of this criticism is misconceived.

29

Whatever insights may be gained from the theory of welfare economics, in fact the literature of market failure has been used largely as a collection of sticks with which to beat the market system. The critics who propose replacing the market system by political decisions rarely address themselves to such crucial matters as the concentration of economic power in political hands, the implications of restriction of choice, the objectives of politicians and administrators, and the quality and extent of knowledge in a society and of its methods of transmission.

7

Critics of the market often argue that people in less developed countries are unable or unwilling to respond to prices and market signals generally. This is not so.

Within the restrictions imposed by governments and the limits set by mores and customs, decision-making by individuals, families and voluntary groups operates in developing countries much as elsewhere. Indeed, because people are on the whole poorer, and therefore weigh up closely the opportunities open to them, they often respond readily, for example, to small price differences and changes. Buyers of scent in Nigeria deliberate whether to buy a tiny bottle or only a drop on the shoulder, or to buy half a cigarette, a single cigarette or a packet of ten cigarettes; or whether to buy a bundle of five matches together with a small striking surface, or to buy a whole box.

In many less developed countries people travel long distances on foot or bicycle or donkey to secure a slightly better price for small lots of produce. In Eastern Nigeria in the 1950s, women selling palm oil would walk or cycle miles to secure another penny or two on the sale of a beer bottle of palm oil, or another shilling on that of a four-gallon tin.

Economic responsiveness does not depend on literacy or formal education. Illiterate, uneducated people can readily recognize an extension of their opportunities, they can tell whether a change makes them better or worse off, and they can certainly tell the difference between more and less.

The economic decisions of individuals in developing countries, as in the West, are circumscribed by their own values and by the mores of the surrounding society. Many millions of Hindu peasants will not slaughter cattle, especially the cow, and are also often reluctant to kill other animals. But they will increase the acreage under crops which have become more profitable, a response recognized in the policies of successive Indian governments. In the West also there are millions of Jews who do not eat pork, and will not do so even if its price falls. And yet they are undeniably capable of responding readily and effectively to economic opportunities.

It is often difficult to predict how people will respond to change, especially to major changes in their own environment. Observers were surprised by the readiness of Asian and African peasants to plant trees and bushes which take several years to produce any income. Conversely, the continued reluctance of millions of Hindus in India to kill animals still comes as a surprise to Westerners, and even to some westernized Indians. The market leaves it to people to take advantage of opportunities or to refuse to do so.

This freedom is denied in proposals for large-scale coercion to remake entire societies and their peoples. Wide moral and political issues are raised by attempts to force people to abandon their traditional beliefs, values, attitudes, mores and modes of living. Governments of developing countries have in fact rarely attempted such enforced transformations. They generally recognize that attempts of this kind would invite strong resistance, possibly revolt. Even substantial moves in such a direction, or suspicions that such attempts will be made, can elicit violent responses, as indeed has often happened in Asia and Africa.

8

I have already said that external market relations have been conspicuous in the advance of the less developed countries. Throughout the less developed world the materially most advanced societies and regions are those with the most commercial contacts with the West, as for instance the cash-crop producing areas in the Far East, West Africa and Latin America; the mineral producing areas of Africa and the Middle East; and the cities and ports throughout the less developed world. This is not surprising. The spread of material progress from more advanced to less advanced areas is a commonplace of economic history.

In recent decades the opportunities and advantages presented by external contacts have been greater than ever before. In the last hundred years the West has provided huge markets for exports and has been a source of knowledge, skills and capital for the less developed world. This wealth of opportunities was not available to the West in its own early stages of development.

Considering the extent and speed of the transformation of much of South-East Asia and West Africa, the process of change was comparatively smooth because it was effected largely through commercial activities. These are activities of people who stake their own resources and those of their supporters. They themselves primarily reap the benefits and bear the losses. They have to consider not only market conditions, including the availability of complementary resources, but also local habits, institutions and susceptibilities. For this reason the disturbing effect of external commercial contacts tends to be gradual and tentative.

Contrast the results of such sequences with the outcome of the Shah's attempts at rapid modernization in Iran – attempts encouraged by teams of economic planners from leading American universities.

Material advance always starts in particular activities and areas. Its outward spread depends on government policies, physical communications and the readiness of people to take advantage of economic opportunities. In all societies, other than the most primitive subsistence economies, there are therefore differences in incomes and rates of progress between individuals, groups and regions. These differences are not reprehensible. They are inevitable. Even in regions where economic advance has been so extensive, as in South-East Asia and West Africa, there are very many people, even entire societies, largely unaffected by this advance, except that they are less afflicted by local wars, slavery, famine and epidemic diseases than they were formerly.

Multinational enterprises have been conspicuous in the rapid economic advance of many developing countries, and antedate their recent prominence in public discourse. They have for centuries

32

played a large part in the shipping, banking, insurance, trading, plantation and mining industries. They were prominent in the establishment of the external commercial contacts of the Third World in the nineteenth and twentieth centuries. The role of multinational merchant firms was crucial in the transformation of South-East Asia and West Africa. Their activities were indispensable in the development of rubber, oil, palm produce, cocoa, groundnuts, coffee and cotton in these regions, products which within a few decades of their establishment became staples of world commerce.

9

The controls which circumscribe or even suppress the market in developing countries are many and varied. The issues they raise differ in their analytical, practical and political interest. I have already touched on some of these controls, and I shall now discuss them further, focussing primarily on matters which I think are less familiar than they deserve to be.

Since about the 1960s, close state economic control has become the order of the day in less developed countries, especially over much of Asia and Africa. The instruments of control include state monopoly of major branches of industry and commerce, notably in the import and export trade, including agricultural exports; numerous state-owned and operated enterprises; official licensing of commercial and industrial activity, including the establishment and operation of businesses; ethnic quotas in employment and in the allocation of licences; comprehensive control over international transactions; restrictions on the external and domestic movement of people, capital and commodities; officially prescribed prices and wages; and large-scale state support to co-operative societies which are in effect extensions of government departments rather than voluntary co-operative societies such as are often seen in the West. Incidents of forced collectivization of agriculture, undisguised confiscation of property, and maltreatment of productive groups unpopular with the rulers have also become more frequent.

Major factors behind the imposition of these controls are familiar from experience in the West. State control of the economy serves the interests of the rulers in many different ways. It increases their hold

33

over the rest of the society. It creates positions of power, prestige and economic benefit to politicians, civil servants and their associates. The controls often also benefit influential private interests by securing lucrative, protected and privileged positions. In the less developed world, especially in Asia and Africa, the difference in political effectiveness between the politicians (including the politicized military), civil servants and their supporters in business and the professions on the one hand, and the population at large on the other hand, is even wider than in the West. These ruling groups are therefore well-placed to promote measures which suit their own personal interests. The operation of some of these controls sets up much greater political tensions in ldcs than in the West for such reasons as the ethnic diversity of their societies, the discrepancy in political power between rulers and subjects, and administrative limitations such as the inability to enforce price control and rationing at the retail level.[11]

Pervasive politicization of life has been a general result of the ubiquitous and extensive economic controls. I have already noted the far-reaching consequences of the politicization of life in less developed countries. I need not, therefore, develop this theme beyond stating that the effects on the population at large have ranged from modest damage to massive hardship and acute suffering.

Besides this politicization of life, state economic controls in ldcs have brought about other damaging results, some of them familiar, others less so. The controls obstruct the movement of people between jobs and places, the establishment of enterprises and the expansion of efficient producers. They inhibit the emergence and spread of experimentation and new ideas, and they retard the erosion of attitudes and customs harmful to material progress.

For obvious reasons, such effects are especially damaging in the relatively early stages of economic development. The adverse effects are particularly pronounced in countries with distinct ethnic groups of differing aptitudes, and where social conditions and natural resources differ widely. The controls invariably restrict severely the volume and diversity of external commercial contacts, contacts which serve as channels not only of skills, capital and commodities, but also of new methods, ideas, wants and crops. The restriction of these contacts correspondingly obstructs the economic opportunities and the economic advance of the population at large. They also affect

34

adversely the terms of trade of farmers, and retard emergence from subsistence production. Extensive controls also much enlarge the scope for corruption.

In most less developed countries, there is a long tradition of the subjection of the individual to the authority of rulers or of custom. The culture of most of Asia and Africa is more authoritarian than in the West (or at any rate than it was formerly in the West), less conducive to self-reliance, sustained curiosity and experimentation. State economic control reinforces the subjection of the individual to authority.

10

The opinions quoted in section 2 above are instances which reflect the suspicion and antagonism of academics, clerics and intellectuals towards the market. These sentiments go hand in hand with disdain for the preferences and habits of ordinary people ('the average sensual man'). Hostility to the market and contempt for ordinary people, which are often only two sides of the same coin, are conspicuous in discussions of the less developed world and its external commercial relations. This is another example illustrating that phenomena and relationships present in the West are especially pronounced in the context of the Third World.

Since the Second World War, articulation of hostility towards the market system has become widespread and pronounced practically everywhere. This reflects the prominence on the contemporary scene of professional politicians, civil servants, academics and media men, and to some extent also of entertainers and churchmen. Between them, these categories in society, often thought of by themselves and others as élites, form the modern political nation; that is, the people whose activities and opinions shape public discussion, even if they are only a small minority of the population.

By and large, the political nation tends to criticize the market order, and whether deliberately or not, provides fuel for its enemies. Replacement of market processes by political decisions provides power, influence, jobs and money for politicians and civil servants. There are also bored, disillusioned and ambitious academics who expect to benefit from such criticism, and from plans and proposals

35

for restricting the scope of the market system. Churchmen manifestly seek a new role for themselves in the face of the erosion of their traditional functions. Increasingly they seem to regard themselves as social welfare officers rather than the spiritual leaders that once they were and still purport to be.

Pressures from within the market system reinforce the activities of these groups in circumscribing or eroding the market. Private sectional interests frequently benefit from more spending and from the imposition of restrictive controls. They therefore routinely organize, act in concert and press for such policies.

The market system provides no mechanism for its own survival. Attempts by firms or individuals to influence the climate of opinion or the overall political situation involve costs in time and money, and occasionally also in unpopularity. Most of these costs are certain and are incurred in the present. They are borne by firms and persons who can expect at best to secure only a small proportion of an uncertain and delayed benefit: few market participants are able or willing to incur these costs.

Success in a market economy requires concentration on concrete problems of production and marketing. Resources accrue to people proficient in these activities and ready to concentrate on them. The required faculties and inclinations do not go well with sustained and perceptive interest in general issues and their analysis. Successful businessmen are not particularly adept at defending the market. Nor have they the time or the inclination to examine the conditions necessary for its survival. Moreover, even if they understand the significance and impact of the relevant arguments, they are still reluctant to find the time required for systematic examination and convincing criticism, for they feel that as individuals they cannot do much to influence the overall situation.

There is, in fact, a curious contrast between the market order and the socialist or communist system. The market system delivers the goods people want, but those who make it work cannot readily explain why it does so. The socialist or communist system does not deliver the goods, but those who operate it can readily explain away its failure. The opponents of the market order are highly articulate and effective. In most countries, political decisions closely affect people's activities, possibly more than ever before. The market order

36

is therefore threatened. An order based on decentralized voluntary decision-making is ill-equipped to face a sustained threat to its own existence. The merits of decentralized decision-making, and the political, social and economic benefits of the market system, will not by themselves ensure that it will survive.

It is probably true that in the West those who broadly favour the market system much outnumber those who oppose it, and also in the aggregate are richer. But preponderance of numbers and of wealth has never been enough to ensure the survival of a nation, society or culture. In spite of its productivity, the market order may well go under unless its participants and supporters have the clarity of thought and the will and courage to work for its survival.

CHAPTER 3

Foreign Aid: Issues and Implications

1

'Foreign aid is the central component of world development.' So in 1981 said Professor Hollis B. Chenery, then Vice President of the World Bank in charge of economic research.[1] How can he have been right? Large-scale development occurs in many places without foreign aid, and did so long before foreign aid was invented.[2]

Official Western aid has now gone to the Third World for about thirty years, more than a human generation. Over this period major deficiencies, even startling anomalies, have become apparent. These untoward results might not matter much if the policy had served to promote development. But it has not done so, and normally cannot do so to any significant extent.

The effects of foreign aid have in fact been quite different. It is foreign aid, for instance, that has brought into existence the Third World (also called the South), and which thus underlies the so-called North–South dialogue or confrontation. Foreign aid is the source of the North–South conflict, not its solution. The paramount significance of aid lies in this very important, perhaps momentous, political result. A further pervasive consequence of aid has been to promote or exacerbate the politicization of life in aid-receiving countries. These major results have been damaging both to the West and to the peoples of the less developed world.

The money spent by the West in no way measures these crucial outcomes. Whatever percentage of their national incomes aid represents, the donor governments cannot wash their hands of the consequences of their so-called caring.

2

What is there in common between, say, Thailand and Mozambique, Nepal and Argentina, India and Chad, Tuvalu and Brazil, Mayotte

38

and Nigeria? Public and political discussion nowadays envisages the world as one-third rich, the West, and two-thirds poor (even hungry), the Third World or South. In this picture, extreme poverty is the common and distinguishing characteristic of the Third World. But there is a continuous range in *per capita* incomes among countries, as is evident from statistics in World Bank publications. The absence of a clear break undermines the concept of a Third World distinguished on the basis of *per capita* incomes from the rest of the world. The place of the line of division between rich and poor countries is quite arbitrary. One could equally well say that the world is two-thirds rich and one-third poor, or one-tenth rich and nine-tenths poor, or choose any other two fractions which add up to one.

The picture is misleading also in that many groups or societies in the Third World, especially in the Far East, the Middle East, South-East Asia and Latin America, are richer than large groups in the West. Nor is the Third World stagnant. Both before and after the Second World War, many Third World countries grew rapidly, including South Korea, Taiwan, Thailand, Malaysia, Singapore, Jordan, Guatemala, Venezuela, Colombia, Brazil, Kenya and the Ivory Coast. Indeed, insofar as global aggregation and averaging of incomes and growth rates make any sense at all, both total and *per capita* incomes in the Third World as a whole have since 1950 probably grown faster than in the West.

But it is hardly sensible to lump together and average the incomes of the very different societies of the Third World or South, which comprise some two-thirds of mankind.[3] Its societies live in widely different physical and social environments, and display radically different attitudes and modes of conduct. Their governments pursue very different policies. The Third World includes millions of aborigines and pygmies, peoples with ancient and sophisticated cultures, and others employing highly advanced methods of business and technology. It is both misleading and condescending to treat the richly varied humanity of the majority of mankind as if it were much of a muchness, or an undifferentiated uniform stagnant mass, which, furthermore, could not emerge from this state without the aid of external donations. The Third World includes, incidentally, micro-states such as Nauru (pop. 6,000), Tuvalu (pop. 10,000) and Mayotte (pop. 20,000), as well as vast countries such as India (pop. 700

million) and the People's Republic of China (pop. 1 billion).

Nor is brotherhood a common characteristic of the Third World, as is evident from the persistent hostility and even armed conflict between many of the countries, including India and Pakistan, Iraq and Iran, Morocco and Algeria, Ethiopia and Somalia, Guatemala and Belize, not to mention the numerous violent internal conflicts. It should not be surprising that attempts at organizing economic co-operation within the Third World have failed – except for co-operation for collective bargaining with the West; and even this is usually organized and financed by the West.

3

The one common characteristic of the Third World is not poverty, stagnation, exploitation, brotherhood or skin colour. It is the receipt of foreign aid. The concept of the Third World and the policy of official aid are inseparable. The one would not exist without the other. The Third World is merely a name for the collection of countries whose governments, with occasional and odd exceptions, demand and receive official aid from the West. Official aid provides the only bond joining together the diverse and often antagonistic constituents. This is currently so, and has been ever since practically all of Asia, Africa and Latin America came to be lumped together in the late 1940s as the underdeveloped world, the non-aligned world, the developing world, the Third World, and now the South. These expressions have never made any sense except to denote a collectivity of aid recipients.

Thus, The Third World is a political and not an economic concept.

To have brought about the Third World has been the most important and far-reaching result of foreign aid. The Third World is moreover a progeny of the West. Aid was introduced and has always been organized by the West. It began with President Truman's Point Four Program of 1949. He urged bold measures to help the underdeveloped countries where, he said, over half of mankind was living in sickness and wretchedness. It was not pressure from the Third World which originated foreign aid. The sequence is exactly the other way round. It was foreign aid which produced the Third World, and it is the Third World which is now a major pressure group for more.

The Third World or the South is simply an entity for engaging in collective bargaining with the West. This has come to be recognized by Third World spokesmen or supporters. For instance, according to the Brandt Report of 1980, the Group of 77 (which by then had 117 member countries) 'represents the solidarity of developing countries which is of historic importance, enabling them to present a common stand, and bring to bear their combined strength in North–South negotiations'.[4]

The West has created an entity hostile to itself – this is the biggest and most intriguing of the many anomalies of aid. Individual Third World countries are often neutral or even friendly to the West, but the organized and articulate Third World is at best critical and more often hostile. The purpose of the Third World *qua* collectivity is to coax or extract money from the West. In view of the West's loss of poise, widespread feelings of guilt and internal dissension, a hostile stance is appropriate for this purpose.

It cannot be doubted that the overriding objective of the Third World (as a collectivity) is to secure large appropriations from the West. This is so even though there are squabbles among some of the recipients over the allocation of aid, and complaints of favouritism against donor countries and the international aid agencies. Such internal disagreements, sometimes vociferous, have not undermined the common front against the West.

Foreign aid also gave birth to the notion of the West (or North) as a single economic decision-making entity, a homogeneous aggregate with identical interests capable of imposing its collective will on the Third World. In fact, Western governments rarely speak or act together in economic matters, least of all in setting market prices. And numerous foreign suppliers compete freely and often fiercely for business in Third World markets. Obvious examples include suppliers of manufactured products such as cars, trucks and chemical products, and construction companies and engineering consultants. Manufacturers and commodity traders compete vigorously in the purchase of exports from the Third World.

Foreign aid has thus created two fictions: the Third World as a substantially uniform collectivity with common interests; and the West as another substantially uniform collectivity, a powerful decision-making unit or homogeneous aggregate manipulating the world economy to the common advantage of its constituents. These fictions have in turn resulted in the reality of the North (that is, the West)–South dialogue or confrontation. References to the modest percentage which foreign aid represents as a proportion of the national income of the donors obscure these pervasive political results.

4

Foreign aid is the transfer of taxpayer's money to distant govern-ments and to the official international organizations.The use of the term aid to describe these transfers pre-empts criticism, obscures issues and prejudges results.

Who could be against aid to the less fortunate? Aid is good, more aid is better. In common parlance, improved aid performance means giving away more money. When aid advocates talk of the disappoint-ing record of aid, they do not mean that aid has been ineffective or damaging, but that there has not been enough of it.

The prevailing uncritical approach to these official wealth trans-fers has allowed startling and often bizarre anomalies to flourish (anomalies in addition to the major anomaly of the West having created a collective rod for its own chastisement). Saudi Arabia, Kuwait, Libya, Iran, Iraq, Bahrain, Vietnam, Cuba and South Yemen all received official Western aid every year from 1977 to 1979. This was at a time when the surpluses of the OPEC countries were widely regarded as embarrassing, even damaging to Western economies, when the government of Vietnam openly persecuted millions of people, and when Cuba despatched troops to Africa, again to the embarrassment of the West.

The survivors among the large numbers of refugees from the aid-recipient Vietnamese government descended on other aid-recipient countries such as the Philippines, Thailand, Indonesia and Malaysia. This influx imposed substantial costs on these governments and greatly increased political tension and conflict. Again, in April 1981, the Secretary General of the United Nations announced special aid of 560 million dollars for African refugees, almost all of whom had fled from governments which continue to receive Western aid.

Substantial transfers have gone and still go to other anti-Western governments besides Vietnam and Cuba; to governments at war with

42

each other; to governments severely restricting the inflow of capital, the shortage of which is said to be the ground for aid; to governments spending lavishly on obvious prestige projects; and to governments pursuing other policies which retard economic advance and harm the interest of their poorest subjects. Another anomaly is large-scale Western aid to governments engaged in the expansion of steel and petrochemical complexes when there is heavy unemployment and much excess capacity in these industries in the West and capacity is being dismantled. Some Western aid is being given directly to establish or enlarge steel capacity in recipient countries. Some British aid has been given to India and Morocco specifically for this purpose. Pressure from construction companies in donor countries is sometimes a factor.

The granting of aid to governments of countries where there are many well-to-do people is also anomalous. The anomaly is exacerbated in the many cases where recipient governments subsidize the consumption of the relatively prosperous. In Mexico, for example, a major aid recipient, the retail price of petrol was for years set by the government at far below what it was in Western Europe, and at less than one-third of the price in the United Kingdom, a major aid donor. All these anomalies clearly could not survive a dispassionate examination of current aid policies. Foreign aid is out of control.

5

Although the case for official wealth transfers is largely taken for granted, various arguments and rationalizations are often advanced. These are addressed primarily to audiences regarded as not yet firmly committed. The principal arguments considered in this chapter fall under the headings of development, poverty and redistribution, exports and employment, political strategy, and restitution.[5]

The central argument for foreign aid has remained that without it Third World countries cannot progress at a reasonable rate, if at all. But not only is such aid patently not required for development: it has tended to obstruct development more than it has promoted it.

External donations have never been necessary for the development of any society anywhere. Economic achievement depends on personal, cultural, social and political factors, that is people's own faculties, motivations and mores, their institutions and the policies of their rulers. In short, economic achievement depends on the conduct of people and their governments.

It diminishes the people of the Third World to suggest that, although they crave for material progress, unlike the West they cannot achieve it without external doles. In fact, of course, large parts of the Third World progressed rapidly long before foreign aid – witness South-East Asia, West Africa and Latin America. The rise of many millions of people from poverty to prosperity in these and other areas of the Third World did not depend on donations from abroad. There are, of course, a number of Third World countries or societies which have not progressed much over the last hundred years. This lack of progress reflects factors which cannot be overcome by aid, but which instead are likely to be reinforced by it.

These conclusions are not surprising. Few private people would persist in giving money to materially unsuccessful or unambitious persons on the ground that this was necessary or helpful for their economic advance.

It should be evident on a little reflection that the volume of investible funds, that is the possession of financial assets or access to them, cannot be a critical determinant of economic development. If it were, large numbers of very poor people could not have attained prosperity in the space of only a few years, as they have done the world over, including for instance the immigrant communities in North America and South-East Asia.

The relative unimportance of the volume of investible funds in material progress has been confirmed by much recent research, including that of Simon Kuznets, Edward Denison, Moses Abramovitz and Sir Alec Cairncross.[6]

The findings of Kuznets and of the other scholars refer very largely to increases in material capital. They apply even more to the significance of the volume of investible funds, because much spending that is termed investment does not result in productive capital formation. Furthermore, the findings refer to the contribution of capital formation to material progress in societies in which social, political and economic conditions were congenial to economic achievement.[7]

Whatever contribution investible funds can make to development can be secured without external donations. This is so because

governments and enterprises in the Third World which can use
capital productively can borrow commercially at home and abroad.[8]
Both before the war and since, the thousands of enterprises in the less
developed world which advanced from very modest beginnings to
considerable size and prosperity readily found the capital necessary
for this process. Similarly, governments of ldcs have been able to
borrow readily, even too readily, from international banks or
through their intermediaries. This has also been true for governments
borrowing to spend on so-called infrastructure, facilities which do not
yield a directly appropriable return. If spending on infrastructure is
productive, it increases taxable capacity so that the governments can
readily service the borrowed capital.

It follows that the absolute maximum contribution to development
of aid transfers is the avoided cost of borrowing, that is interest and
amortization charges. As a percentage of the national income of
large Third World countries, this maximum contribution is at best far
too small to register in national aggregative statistics. For India in
recent years, it would have been of the order of one-quarter to one-
half per cent of recorded GNP.

Foreign aid can thus do no more for development than to reduce
somewhat the cost of a resource which is not a major independent
factor in economic development.

Suppose, however, that, contrary to the results of reflection and
observation, the volume and cost of investible funds were critical
determinants of economic advance. Then the actions of many Third
World governments which restrict the inflow of foreign private
capital, a policy facilitated or even made possible by the receipt of
aid, would show that these governments do not care much for
economic development. The same applies to the practice of some
governments, including those of India and Nigeria, of passing on to
other governments part of the aid they themselves receive.

Any benefit to development from the reduction of the cost of
investible funds is likely to be modest, even minimal. It is also likely
to be much more than offset by the adverse repercussions of aid. Two
significant considerations or asymmetries are pertinent in assessing
the benefits and costs for development of the inflow of aid.

First, most of the adverse repercussions, including the most
significant effects, operate on personal, social and political factors

45

which, unlike the volume and cost of investible funds, are critical determinants of material progress. Second, as we shall see shortly, the adverse repercussions are brought about by even comparatively small amounts of official aid.

To begin with the most important adverse result. Official wealth transfers increase the resources and power of recipient governments compared with the rest of the society. Official transfers enhance the hold of governments over their subjects, and promote the politicization of life. The untoward, even disastrous consequences of this politicization have already been examined in Chapter 2 above, including the consequences for economic performance and progress. Official aid has not been the sole cause of this politicization, but it has often been a significant contributory factor.

There are further harmful implications and repercussions of foreign aid which are far from trivial. Aid helps or even enables governments to pursue policies which patently retard growth and exacerbate poverty. There is a long list of such policies, which includes persecution of the most productive groups, especially minorities, and sometimes their expulsion; restraints on the activities of traders and even the destruction of the trading system; restriction of the inflow of foreign capital, enterprise and skills; voluntary or compulsory purchase of foreign enterprises (which deprives the country of skills very helpful to development, besides absorbing scarce capital); forced collectivization; price policies which discourage food production; and, generally, the imposition of economic controls which restrict external contacts and domestic mobility and so retard the spread of new ideas and methods. But even where, as is rarely the case, damaging policies are not pursued, efforts to obtain aid are apt to divert attention from the basic conditions of development and the possibility of influencing them favourably.

Aid is also apt to bias development policy towards unsuitable external models. Familiar examples include steel and petrochemical complexes and official airlines. Moreover, in some instances the adoption of external prototypes has gone hand in hand with attempts at more comprehensive modernization, including the attempted transformation of people's mores and values and their institutions.

As we have seen earlier in this section, the maximum contribution of aid to development cannot exceed the reduction of the cost of investible funds as percentage of gross domestic product of the recipient countries. The various adverse repercussions, on the other hand, are brought about by amounts of aid which, while small as a percentage of the gross domestic product of recipient countries, are often a significant part of government revenues and of foreign exchange earnings. These are the relevant magnitudes in this context, because aid goes to governments, not to the population at large, and increases both the revenues and the external balances at their direct disposal.

Aid, necessarily, is significantly larger relative to tax receipts and foreign exchange earnings than it is to the national income of a recipient country. The differences in the ratios can be striking. Here are the 1980 ratios (the latest available) for India and Tanzania, leading aid recipients in Asia and Africa respectively.[9] For India, aid was 1.6 per cent of recorded GNP, 16.8 per cent of tax receipts and 31.2 per cent of export earnings. For Tanzania, the corresponding figures were 18.1 per cent, 106.8 per cent and 152.8 per cent.

The repercussions of aid cannot be assessed in terms of the ratio of aid to GNP or, as is sometimes done, the ratio of aid to total investible funds in a recipient country.[10]

6

The progress of some aid recipients is often instanced to show the usefulness of aid. At first sight this may seem to be telling evidence, but it is in fact irrelevant. As we have seen, the contribution of aid cannot exceed the avoided cost of investible funds, the volume of which is not a significant determinant of Third World development. And as we have also noted, many poor countries in the Third World advanced very rapidly long before the invention of aid.

The establishment and success of individual (so-called) development projects financed by aid are also often instanced as evidence of the effectiveness of aid. This again is irrelevant as evidence. When such projects promise to be productive, they can be financed by government or private enterprise so that the contribution of aid is again only the avoided cost of borrowing. The idea that without foreign aid such activities could not have taken place is unwarranted, as is evident from history throughout the Third World: witness for

47

example the plantations, mining, manufacturing and transport undertakings established by private capital in Asia, Africa and Latin America long before the availability of foreign aid. And privately financed projects are much more likely to be productive than aid-financed schemes because they are more closely geared to market conditions and to the surrounding social scene.

Much more informative is the evidence provided by the difficulties of many Third World aid recipients in servicing their debts: the burden of Third World indebtedness is a persistent theme of the aid lobbies. Insofar as the debt burden is unmanageable, such difficulties would imply that the investible funds have been ineffective or counter-productive as instruments for development, or that the public finances have been mismanaged. This is highlighted by the little-appreciated fact that the interest burden on the outstanding debt of the great bulk of Third World countries has ranged from 0.4 per cent to 1.1 per cent of their combined GNP over the decade 1970–79.[11] Moreover, by historic standards, both total indebtedness and debt obligations in relation to exports have not been unusually high even in recent years.[12]

For many years now, a substantial proportion of total Third World indebtedness has been in the form of soft loans with large grant elements under aid agreements. In 1979 this proportion was over 40 per cent, and in 1980 it was about 80 per cent.[13] There was a substantial increase in Third World debts to the Western banks in the 1970s, and this is often blamed now for the financial problems of many ldcs. It is usually forgotten that it has always been a central argument of aid advocates that aid is necessary because ldcs are unable to secure capital from commercial sources.

The burden of Third World indebtedness has been much reduced both by the general rise in money values and by earlier postponements and write-offs.[14] Over all but a very short period, these developments have more than offset such recent changes as the increase in nominal interest rates or in the international value of the US dollar. Incidentally, aid cancellations, rescheduling or other financial rewards to governments unable or unwilling to honour their obligations amount to preferential treatment of the incompetent, the improvident or the dishonest. This is unlikely to promote behaviour helpful to economic progress. The general economic plight of many aid recipients after decades of aid also points to its ineffectiveness.

The success of the Marshall Plan in the early post-war years is frequently invoked in support of wealth transfers to the Third World. This analogy is altogether misleading. The damaged economies of Western Europe had to be revived, not developed. As was evident from pre-war experience, the personal, social and political factors congenial to economic achievement were present. Recent research has shown, moreover, that Marshall aid played at best a minor part in the recovery of the economy of the Federal Republic of Germany.[15] This finding accords with expectations, for reasons set out in section 5 above. In any event, within four years Marshall aid to Europe could be terminated, and Germany became both an exporter of capital and also a major source of foreign aid. Contrast this with suggestions that official aid to the Third World will have to continue for a long time, at least into the twenty-first century.

It is paradoxical to suggest that aid begun in the mid-1950s will have to be continued into the twenty-first century, or even further. Aid for development has been canvassed as necessary to decrease the dependence of Third World countries on the West. Inasmuch as aid cannot contribute significantly to development, the matter is misconceived. Worse still, aid has made it possible for governments to pursue such policies as subsidized import substitution, forced collectivization, price policies which inhibit agricultural production both for local consumption and for export, inflationary financial policies, and the maintenance of over-valued exchange rates. Besides damaging the interests of the population at large and aggravating poverty, these policies have also increased the demand for imports, while simultaneously decreasing the ability to pay for them. These countries have been made more rather than less dependent on the West and its largesse.

7

Relief of poverty in the Third World is the second major proclaimed purpose of aid. It is this objective which most appeals to genuinely compassionate people in the West.

Foreign aid does not in fact go to the pitiable figures we see on aid posters, in aid advertisements, and in other aid propaganda in the media. It goes to the governments, that is to the rulers, and the policies of the rulers who receive aid are sometimes directly responsible for conditions such as those depicted. But even in less extreme instances, it is still the case that aid goes to the rulers; and their policies, including the pattern of public spending, are determined by their own personal and political interests, among which the position of the poorest has very low priority.[16]

Indeed, to support rulers on the basis of the poverty of their subjects does nothing to discourage policies of impoverishment. As already noted, many Third World governments have persecuted and even expelled some of the most productive groups, including Chinese in Vietnam and Indonesia, or Asians in East Africa, not to speak of Europeans. On the criterion of poverty such governments qualify for more aid, because incomes in their countries are now lower. The more damaging the policies the more acute becomes the need, and therefore the more effective appeals for aid by governments based on the poverty or need of their subjects. This is but one example that poverty cannot be discussed sensibly without looking at its background.

These anomalies or paradoxes are obscured when it is suggested that giving money to the rulers of poor countries is the same as giving it to poor, even destitute people. To give money to governments is certainly not the same thing as helping the poor. To overlook the distinction is an example of the practice of identifying the government with the people at large, treating a collectivity as if it were a single decision-making unit, or a homogeneous aggregate of components with identical interests.

Western aid to Third World governments, especially in Asia and Africa, has extensively supported policies which have aggravated the lot of the poorest. In Tanzania, a major aid recipient, government policies have greatly discouraged food production. President Mobutu of Zaire, another large aid recipient, has expelled large numbers of traders, and this has led to enforced reversion to subsistence production over large areas, causing much hardship and deprivation.

We may also note some less extreme instances. Lavish spending on show projects by aid-recipient governments is familiar throughout the Third World. How do the poorest benefit from the creation at vast expense of brand new capitals such as Brasilia, Islamabad, Abuja in Nigeria,[17] Lilongwe in Malawi, or Dodoma in Tanzania?[18] Or from international airlines throughout the Third World, including countries such as Burundi and Laos, where the vast majority of people does not use them and local people cannot operate them? It does not help the poor in Zaire or Ghana that these countries have international airlines with elegant offices in the West End of London and elsewhere. Many of these projects and enterprises facilitated by the flow of foreign aid represent a drain on domestic resources and have to be subsidized by local taxpayers.[19] The huge expenditure on arms by Third World governments, intended mostly for use against other Third World countries or against their own subjects, is also pertinent. Third World governments account for about one-fifth of total world expenditure on armaments.[20] These are but a few examples of radical differences between foreign aid rhetoric and Third World reality.

There are many rich people in the aid-recipient countries of Asia, Africa and Latin America. Enterprises and individuals from the Third World often buy large stakes in Western companies.[21] Since about 1979 individual Nigerian buyers have been prominent in the market for prime properties in London. Some London estate agents have sent envoys to that country, whose government has for many years regularly been receiving substantial Western aid.

Large-scale spending on show projects, and the presence of large numbers of rich people in ldcs in which there are many extremely poor people, make it clear that the rulers, while demanding external donations in the name of international redistribution, are not particularly interested in domestic policies to help their poor. They are interested in such policies only if they serve to benefit their own personal and political purposes, as for instance expropriation of the wealth of their political opponents, or of politically unpopular groups. Other forms of redistribution do not usually accord with local mores, and machinery for this purpose or for state relief of poverty often does not exist.

What is pertinent in all this is that while foreign aid can do little or nothing for development or relief of poverty, the receipt of aid can relieve immediate shortages and alleviate difficult situations. It enables governments to pursue even extremely damaging policies for

51

years on end because the inflow of funds conceals from the population at least temporarily some of the worst effects of their policies. To take but one example, it has been widely and rightly recognized even by supporters of President Nyerere that without large-scale external aid he would not have been able to persist for so many years with forced collectivization and large-scale removal of people into so-called socialist villages.

Would it be possible for the donor countries to help the poor either by influencing the policies of the aid-recipient governments, or by giving aid directly to the poorest instead of to their rulers? Neither course is practicable as such attempts would be resisted and sabotaged by the governments. Both Western charities and official aid organizations already encounter difficulties in some countries. But were it practicable to give official aid directly to the poorest, other problems would arise, many of them well-nigh intractable.

The most obvious of these problems is the pauperization and de-skilling of the recipients. In the Third World very large numbers of the poorest people are materially unambitious. In much the same way as most other people, they usually like to have more of the good things of life. But for valid reasons, many of them may not be prepared to give up their established ways of living. Official donations from abroad are likely to turn these poor into paupers, so that these grants may have to be continued indefinitely. Whole societies can thus be pauperized. A recent example which is informative although extreme is the large-scale pauperization in the United States trust territory of Micronesia.[22] A somewhat similar result has been produced by the protracted subsidies to the Navaho Indians by the United States Federal Government.

8

'Exactly the same for everybody – that's how it must be.' This sentence is part of the peroration in an illustrated booklet published in 1982 for mass distribution to schoolchildren by the West German government department responsible for foreign aid.[23]

This sentiment is shared by many people who regard foreign aid as the advent of global redistribution. They envisage aid as a natural extension of internal redistributive taxation from the national to the international plane, that is, as the global application of egalitarianism. If this idea were to be accepted and implemented on a large scale, aid would in the future have additional political, social and economic consequences at least as serious as those it has had hitherto.

An initial point to be stressed is that international aid transfers differ radically from internal transfers by means of progressive taxation, whatever the case for the latter. Unlike progressive taxation, aid transfers are in no way adjusted to the personal circumstances of taxpayers and recipients. Many donor taxpayers are far poorer than many people in recipient countries where much aid benefits the powerful and the relatively well-off.

Redistributive taxation postulates basic similarities of conditions, and therefore of requirements, within its area of operation. The meaning of riches and poverty depends crucially on people's requirements, and thus on physical and social living conditions. Globally, these requirements differ widely. This is obvious for physical conditions, notably climate. But it applies also to social conditions including customs and values.

How should we rank for purposes of redistribution a recipient of welfare payments in the West, an African chief, a Buddhist monk in the East, and the headman of a New Guinea tribe living in Stone Age conditions? On the basis of income the first would be richest. Nevertheless, he is regarded as poor by his fellow countrymen, while the others are regarded locally as men of prominence and of substance. It is also questionable whether people in the West should be taxed for the benefit of the governments of societies where people refuse to kill animals, as in India, or let women take paid work, as in many Moslem countries; or for the benefit of governments which pursue policies plainly detrimental to their people's welfare.

Attempts to reduce appreciable international differences in income would have to involve extensive coercion. This is because of the wide differences in the physical and social conditions in different countries, and also in the operation of the underlying determinants of economic performance. To bring about anything approaching worldwide equality of incomes would require world government with totalitarian powers used far more ruthlessly than by totalitarian governments in particular countries.

Unlike progressive taxation within a country, global redistribution

53

relies on international income comparisons. These are subject to a wide range of error, and they greatly understate the relative incomes of large Asian and African countries by comparison with the West. According to World Bank estimates, the official figure of the national income of India has to be raised by a factor of more than three to make it comparable to that of the United States. Other scholarly studies have found much larger biases and errors. They arise for such reasons as the use in these comparisons of official exchange rates instead of purchasing power parities; underestimation (or complete disregard) of much subsistence production; and the neglect of differences in age composition between the West and the Third World. Such considerations, incidentally, also help to put into perspective statistics of Third World incomes and changes in incomes which purport to be estimates to within fractions of one per cent.

Because international income differences reflect people's attributes, mores, institutions and political arrangements, any politically organized reduction in income differences is likely to be temporary, because the basic factors behind international income differences tend to reassert themselves. The process may therefore need to be continued indefinitely. Global redistribution also implies transfers from more productive to less productive people, and thereby reduces overall productivity of resources.

In assessing the redistributive results of international wealth transfers, it must be remembered that they necessarily involve costs of administration which at times are large. Recent events in the Food and Agricultural Organization of the United Nations (FAO) are discussed in the next chapter.

9

Foreign aid is often advocated as helpful or even necessary for Western prosperity. It is claimed that aid increases purchasing power and advances growth in the Third World, and thereby promotes exports and employment in the West. This is an argument most often addressed to businessmen and trade unionists, and it is a major theme of the Brandt Report.

This claim is invalid. It would be invalid even if the transfers significantly promoted development in the Third World (which,

54

however, they cannot do). Exports bought with the proceeds of foreign aid are given away. It is sophistry to say that people who give away part of their wealth must be better off because those whom they have helped are better off or will be better off. A businessman does not prosper by donating money to people some of whom may later purchase his products with part of it. This is not to deny that sectional interests in the donor countries often benefit from the expenditure of aid.

The provision of ships by Britain to India, Poland and Vietnam in the 1970s benefited labour and management in British shipyards. But the shipyards could have been used at government expense for other purposes; or the government expenditure could have been used for other forms of so-called employment creation.

It is sophistry also to say that large-scale aid to the Third World will alleviate unemployment, recession and de-industrialization in the West. If it were really possible to cure or relieve unemployment or recession by more government spending, this could be done more effectively by Western countries at home by spending, for example, on the modernization of industry and the improvement of the infrastructure, or on industrial or regional subsidies, defence, social services or personal subsidies. Altogether, state spending to increase employment is more effective if it is disbursed directly at home, rather than to distant governments abroad. Moreover, any products created by domestic spending remain in the donor countries.

Indeed, official aid can aggravate unemployment in the donor countries. Insofar as foreign aid diminishes the volume of productive investible funds in the donor countries, it reduces employment opportunities and incomes. Again, by subsidizing industries in the Third World it may enable them to compete directly with industries in the donor countries, including some in which there is already unemployment and excess capacity.

Moreover, aid often adds to the balance of payments difficulties of donors, a result which encourages or requires restrictive financial policies quite apart from the effects of the taxation required to pay for aid. In sum, the idea that aid helps the economies of the donors simply ignores the cost of the resources given away.

10

A political argument favoured especially in the United States is that without large-scale aid the Third World will drift into the Soviet camp. This argument also is insubstantial.

To begin with, about one-third of all Western aid is channelled through official international agencies. In the allocation of funds, these organizations are not permitted to take into account the political interests of donors. Moreover, the Soviet Union is represented in the United Nations and can thus affect the direction of substantial multilateral transfers under United Nations programmes, though its own financial contribution is negligible. Indeed, practically the entire Soviet non-military aid is channelled to client-states, notably Cuba, North Korea, Vietnam, South Yemen, Ethiopia and Afghanistan, most of which have also received aid from the West.

Western political interests are also largely ignored in direct transfers between donor and recipient governments. Aid administrators are not qualified either by training or often by inclination to act as promoters of Western political interests. Much aid is given regardless of the political conduct of the recipients, or of their political and military significance. It often arouses the resentment of the recipients when they do not receive as much as they want or feel entitled to. And they often oppose the donors to assert their own independence. Official transfers have also often helped to bring to the fore governments hostile to the market system and sympathetic to the Soviet ideology. This is because aid goes directly to governments and, as we have already noted, tends to politicize life in the recipient countries. This effect is reinforced by the preference of many influential aid advocates and administrators for governments trying to run closely controlled economies.

Since the earliest days of aid, many recipients have been vocal in their opposition to the Western donors whom they have denigrated and thwarted as best they could. Examples range from Nkrumah in the 1950s to Gadaffi, Nyerere and Mengistu in the 1980s.

Many Third World governments derive their aid from the West, but their ideology and political stance from the East.

11

Many people, especially in the Third World but also in the West, think of aid as restitution or partial restitution for past wrongs.

What are these supposed wrongs? Contact with the West has been the prime agent of material progress in the Third World. Material achievement in the less developed world diminishes as one moves away from the foci of Western impact. The poorest and most backward are the populations with few or no external contacts. To say that commercial contacts damage the Third World is to suggest that people in these countries do not know either what they are about or what is good for them when they buy imported goods, or when they produce crops for export.

The notion that Western prosperity has been achieved at the expense of the Third World is a variant of the familiar misconception that the incomes of prosperous people have been extracted from the less well-off. In fact incomes are normally earned, that is produced, by the recipients.

The notion that the West has progressed and prospered at the expense of the Third World is not only unfounded, but also harmful. It lends spurious plausibility to damaging official restrictions on external contacts imposed by Third World governments. Moreover, the notion spills over in domestic discussions in the Third World. It inspires sentiments and policies directed against economically productive but politically unpopular and ineffective groups.

The most familiar specific arguments in support of aid as compensation or restitution are unfounded. For instance, the much-canvassed idea that the West manipulates prices to the detriment of the Third World misconceives market operations. Prices in international markets are the outcome of myriads of individual transactions and decisions; they are not set by an organization called the West. (If they were imposed by the West, why are Third World export prices ever allowed to rise in real terms?) In any case, even if the terms of trade of the South were unfavourable on some criterion or other, this would mean only that the South had not benefited as much from its contacts with the West as it would have done had prices been more favourable. The peoples of the South are certainly better

57

off than if they had no trade to have terms about. As it happens, the terms of trade of most Third World countries with the West have been unusually favourable in recent decades. The overall external purchasing power of these countries' exports over Western goods has been far greater than ever before.

And what about colonialism? Most Western aid donors, including the United States (much the largest donor), never had colonies of any significance. Some of them, including America, Canada, Australia and New Zealand, were themselves British colonies. And whatever its objectionable features, nineteenth- and twentieth-century colonialism, which is what is meant by colonialism in this context, was of great economic benefit to the people of these countries. For instance, Ethiopia and Liberia, which were not colonies, are among the most backward countries in Africa. Much the same is true of Asia – witness Bhutan, Sikkim, Tibet and Nepal. And as noted in Chapter 2, the much-maligned multinational companies, alleged instruments of neo-colonialism, are absent in the poorest countries and regions.

Orwell's Newspeak is rife here. For instance, according to UNCTAD General Principle XIV, passed by an overwhelming majority at UNCTAD in 1964, colonialism is incompatible with material progress. This was announced at a time when Hong Kong, the last remaining sizeable Western colony in the Far East, was progressing so rapidly that Western countries were imposing controls on imports from it to protect their own domestic industries. The idea that colonial status precludes material progress is refuted by obvious evidence from all over the world.

What about the Atlantic slave trade? Most Western countries were not involved in it at all. Asian countries, the largest foreign aid recipients, were unaffected. And horrible and destructive as this trade was, it was not a cause of African backwardness. The region most affected, namely West Africa, had by 1914 become the most advanced part of Black Africa.[24] Incidentally, the Arab slave trade, which began before Atlantic slavery and far outlasted it, was even more horrible and was stopped by Western efforts. But the Arab slave trade is practically never mentioned in this context. The West has a monopoly both of guilt and of the obligation to make restitution.

The relative prosperity of the West compared to the less developed world is at times adduced as a ground for restitution. Thus it is suggested that Western prosperity must have been achieved at the expense of the Third World; or that this prosperity has obstructed and still obstructs the advance of less developed countries; or that international income differences are damaging to the self-respect of people in the less developed world. In these arguments, the case for aid as restitution merges into the case for redistribution.

However, these arguments are once again spurious. The West has plainly not caused the poverty of the Third World. And the relative prosperity of some societies is neither surprising nor reprehensible. Some people have always emerged from the poverty surrounding them sooner or to a greater extent than have others. But this earlier emergence usually helps rather than obstructs the position and prospects of those who are still poor.

12

So far we have been considering what may be called the major components in the advocacy of foreign aid until the early 1970s. But new arguments for aid sprout with regularity. Here we take a brief look at three more recent arrivals.

Population growth is not a significant obstacle to material progress, which depends on people and their social and political arrangements, not on investible funds or physical resources per head. This is evident from the prosperity of densely populated countries both in the Third World and in the West, in the past and at present.[25]

A recent argument for large-scale aid is based on the much-increased cost of oil. High oil prices are said to have blighted the development prospects of many Third World countries. According to this argument, these countries cannot emerge from poverty and misery or develop satisfactorily unless they receive more aid to compensate them for the increased cost of oil. Yet South Korea, Taiwan, Hong Kong, Singapore, Brazil and many other Third World countries have continued to prosper in recent years, although they import all or practically all of their oil. Moreover, the yet more recent decline in the price of oil has provoked a new argument for aid: some of the oil-producing ldcs are said to merit additional aid because their export earnings have been reduced. It is not surprising, however, that

59

no one seems to have advocated a reduction in the flow of aid to oil-importing ldcs. In fact, larger flows of Western aid have sometimes been advocated on the grounds that aid to them from the richer oil-producing ldcs has been or is likely to be curtailed.

Since 1980, yet another argument for foreign aid has become prominent. According to this, without continuing or additional aid, Third World debtors would default on their obligations to Western banks, which would lead to financial crisis or even collapse. However, if it is deemed desirable or necessary to bail out the banks with taxpayers' money (which is doubtful), they should be rescued directly, and not by giving money to the debtors who may not even use it to meet their obligations. This particular argument is a variant of one noted earlier, namely that the donor countries benefit from exports bought with foreign aid which they themselves have provided.

This argument is the latest in a long line of rationalizations for foreign aid. It will not be the last.[26] The level of income, rate of development (rapid, slow or negative), condition of particular groups of people in ldcs, and changes in export and import prices have all been pressed into the service of the cause, besides many other circumstances, either real or fictitious, relevant or irrelevant. The financial, political and emotional interests behind foreign aid will help to ensure that these rationalizations will persist and others will be put forward. These considerations help to explain why foreign aid has increased steadily and substantially over the years: 'The level of aid flows has grown rapidly in the past two decades, even allowing for inflation. In 1980 it equalled $36 billion, a real growth of about 4 per cent annually since 1960.'[27]

13

As already noted, foreign aid cannot achieve its declared objectives, and has far-reaching damaging political and economic results. Yet it will not be terminated promptly because of existing commitments, and because of the vested interests behind it both in the government and the market sectors, in donor as well as in recipient countries.

Can the worst effects of aid be mitigated by changes in its methods of operation?

To begin with, it might help a little if aid were to take forms which made it possible to identify its costs and possibly its benefits. This rules out indirect methods of aid such as commodity agreements. Not only are their results perverse, but their overall impact cannot be assessed.[28] And such schemes are not subject to any form of public budgetary control.

There would be a strong case for replacing soft loans by outright grants. The latter avoids problems of measurement and the confusion between gifts and loans. Since the late 1970s, a large proportion of soft loans from the West to the Third World were already grants in all but name, with a grant element often exceeding over ninety per cent, quite apart from the high probability of the effects of prospective inflation, rescheduling and default.[29] Aid should also take the form of direct grants from donor government to recipient government, rather than of payments to multilateral organizations, in turn to be distributed by them to the ultimate recipients. Direct grants allow a modicum of control by the elected representatives of the taxpayers in the donor countries, that is the real donors. Attempts to extend the multilateral component of aid should be resisted. The same applies to proposals to make aid more automatic by the introduction of international taxation, as proposed in the Brandt Report.[30]

But these and other reforms would make little difference in practice unless the granting of aid were made deliberately discriminating. Aid would have to be concentrated carefully on governments whose domestic and external policies were most likely to promote the general welfare of their people, notably their economic progress. Aid would have to go to governments which tried to achieve this end by effective administration, the performance of the essential tasks of government, and the pursuit of liberal economic policies. At present, many aid-recipient governments neglect even such basic tasks as maintaining public security while nevertheless trying to run closely controlled economies. Selective allocation of aid along these lines would reduce its propensity to politicize life, and thereby reduce the extent and intensity of political conflict. It would also promote prosperity in the recipient countries, to the limited extent that external donations can do so.

Voluntary agencies, notably non-politicized charities, already do much for the humanitarian relief of poverty in the Third World. They could do much more if it were recognized that relief of need belongs to their sphere. In this realm, the international comity among countries calls for official aid only to meet unforeseeable and exceptional disasters.

As for economic development, the West can best promote this by the reduction of its often severe barriers to imports from poor countries. External commerce is an effective stimulus to economic progress. It is commercial intercourse with the West which has transformed economic life in the Far East, South-East Asia, and parts of Africa and Latin America.

However, even removal of trade restrictions may well do little for the economic advance of some Third World countries and groups. But where the enlargement of external opportunities would not bring about the economic advance of particular societies, external donations to their governments would be even less likely to achieve this result.

CHAPTER 4

Multinational Aid:
an Improvement?

1

The consensus view is that aid is necessary for the promotion of development in the less developed world and for the relief of poverty there. This view applies to so-called bilateral aid as well as to so-called multilateral aid. I shall henceforth refer to bilateral aid as national aid, and to multilateral aid as multinational aid. I do so because the usual terms, especially the former, are misleading in that they imply reciprocity between donors and recipients. But all aid is unilateral in the sense that the donors give resources and the recipients are not obliged to give anything in return.

As explained in some detail in the preceding chapter, the consensus view on aid is mistaken.

Since the mid-1960s, advocates of aid have insisted that aid would be much more effective if it were multinational. The reasoning behind this view is conveniently illustrated in these quotations from the Pearson Report of 1969 and the World Bank publication *IDA in Retrospect* of 1982:

Bilateral assistance inevitably means unequal geographical preferences in aid distribution. In order to assure that all developing countries whose performance and level of development warrants it receive the development assistance which they can effectively absorb, the resources available to international organizations must be considerably expanded. It is only with such greatly enlarged resources that international development agencies can play a significant role in offsetting the distortions caused by bilateral allocation criteria.[1]

International agencies have an important part to play in facilitating regional integration among developing countries. The potential gains from closer co-operation of this kind are very large, and in many cases some form of economic integration seems indispensable to economic viability. International organizations and especially regional agencies and development banks are often at present the standard bearers of integration.[2]

The proliferation of multilateral agencies during the 1970s reflected the view that there were certain things multilaterals could do better than countries acting alone. Multilaterals are still seen as being more effective in influencing economic policies in developing countries, perhaps because their advice is seen as being disinterested and apolitical. They have become specialists in preparing and financing sound, long-term development projects having clear economic benefits.[3]

We shall show, on the contrary, that multinationalization does not increase the productivity of aid. Neither does it remove its short-comings, nor put an end to the many anomalies that have attended it. Rather, it aggravates its defects. Nevertheless, the advocacy of multinational aid has been successful. The multinational component in Western aid has increased from negligible amounts in the early 1950s to about 13 per cent of the total in 1960, and to about 35 per cent in 1980.

2

The main thrust of the advocacy of multinational aid is that it is more objective than national aid, and therefore more effective. It is said to have the merit that it is outside politics and, in particular, short-term political considerations; that it is administered by disinterested experts; and that it is not affected by the donors' national interests (i.e. it is not distorted, as its advocates would put it).

Aid represents taxpayers' money given to foreign governments, whether directly or through the international agencies. In this sense, aid cannot but be political.

Nevertheless, foreign aid is widely regarded as being above party political debate in Western Europe, and to a lesser extent in the United States. In Britain, this special status has often been specific-ally stated by spokesmen for the major political parties. The same non-party approach prevails throughout Western Europe, including Western Germany which is often regarded as a hard-liner in international economic relations.[4] It is thus not the case that the flow of national aid from the major donors is materially affected by the vagaries of political fashion or by the outcomes of elections.

Multinationalization of aid does not depoliticize it. It substitutes political control by the international organizations for political control by the donor government over national aid. In practice, much of this latter control admittedly is nominal, but vestiges remain. (In practice, of course, taxpayers' control is yet more remote and ineffective.)

The international aid organizations and their staffs are not disinterested, as their supporters are apt to assert. It is true that their interests may not be the same as those of the donor countries and their taxpayers. But like other large organizations, international aid organizations (that is, their delegates and their bureaucracies) tend to work for the expansion of the volume and scope of their activities and the size of their budgets. Delegates to the international organizations derive status and perquisites. This is particularly important for Third World representatives who form the great majority in most international organizations. Staff members of the organizations have their own political and financial interests. Multinational aid provides well-paid and influential positions, both within these organizations and elsewhere. Moreover, the staff members are apt to think of themselves as agents of the member governments, the great majority of which are from the Third World. On this ground also, the inclinations and interests of the staff members are best served by more multinational aid and by support of the policies favoured by these governments, although the policies often conflict with the welfare of their own peoples or the interests of the Western donors.

In any case, it has become received doctrine since the early 1970s that international organizations should not make their aid allocations contingent upon the policies of the recipients. The celebrated United Nations Declaration for the Establishment of the New International Economic Order in 1974 stated clearly that 'every country [i.e. government] has the right to adopt the economic and social system that it deems to be the most appropriate for its own development and not to be subjected to discrimination of any kind as a result'. This means that whatever a government might do, it should not be penalized and its entitlement to aid should not be affected. Thus, for example, Third World governments are apt to favour state-controlled economies. And yet, among other damaging consequences the extension of state controls promotes politicization of life and its concomitant tensions and conflicts. It also serves to divert attention and resources from productive economic activity to preoccupation with politics, and with the outcome of political and administrative decisions; and it encourages the restriction of external

65

commercial contacts. Nevertheless, the international aid organizations are not likely to resist these policies, because this would be regarded as inappropriate interference in the domestic arrangements of the recipient governments. It is unlikely also because many staff members of the international organizations favour *dirigiste* policies, on grounds of both self-interest and political inclination.

These characteristics of multinational aid go unrecognized in the argument that multinational aid is more effective than national aid in promoting development or relieving poverty. But it is not surprising that both in public and private spending the more distant the relationship between those who supply funds and those who use them the more likely it is that the funds will not be used effectively for the pursuit of their avowed purposes. In multinational aid there is no contact at all between the donors (the taxpayers) and the spenders (the aid administrators and recipient governments).

A further argument in favour of multinational aid as compared with national aid can be dealt with briefly. National aid is often criticized because much of it may be tied to supplies from the donor countries. However, such tying simply reduces the real value of the aid below the nominal value. It affects the statistics of the value of the resources transferred, but not the reality of the transfer.

3

The major strands in the preceding critical examination of the arguments for multinational aid are amply supported by events. Here are some examples.

The impotence of individual donors over the disposition of multinational aid to which they have contributed was graphically brought home at the time of the Falklands War. Although at war, Britain was obliged to give aid to Argentina because it was a participant in the United Nations Development Programme. British objections to the continuation of this aid were unavailing.[5]

Again, British national aid to President Amin of Uganda was gradually run down in the mid-1970s, and was almost completely eliminated some years before his overthrow. Substantial EEC aid, on the other hand, continued to be allocated to him throughout his rule, once more in the face of British opposition.

The Food and Agriculture Organization of the United Nations (FAO) is the largest of the UN specialized agencies and a major aid organization. In November 1981, 152 states were members. Decisions are made on a one-state one-vote basis. When the budget for 1982 and 1983 was debated at the FAO's conference in Rome in November 1981, the major contributors opposed the budget proposals drawn up by the Director General. Five member countries – the United States, Britain, West Germany, Japan and Switzerland, between them responsible for 54 per cent of total contributions – voted against the proposals. Another nine, responsible for about 10 per cent, abstained. The proposals were carried by the votes of the remaining 110 countries, 92 of whom accounted for 1.4 per cent of total contributions, each contributing between 0.01 and 0.05 per cent. Several were in arrears with their contributions.

The major donor-members had three main objections. First, the proposals were for a large increase in the total budget of about one-third in terms of US dollars. Second, the bulk of the budget was to be spent on administrative costs, primarily in Italy (two-thirds of the total regular budget, according to one report). Third, there was a total lack of external control over, or assessment of, the programmes carried out by the FAO itself or financed by it. There had been – as there still is – strong and successful opposition within the FAO to such external assessments, whether carried out by donor countries or by other international organizations. Opposition came from the staff, including the Director General, who regarded such assessment as inappropriate and impracticable.[6] It also came from many of the recipient governments which were unwilling to have their own activities associated with FAO programmes examined by outsiders, and from some donor governments which, for various reasons, supported this stance of the FAO staff and the recipients of its largesse.[7] There is much truth in Professor Thomas Sowell's observation that the poor are a gold-mine.

The major donors could do nothing although they supplied most of the funds. Yet none withdrew from the organization. This may be thought the more remarkable in that they were being subjected to virulent verbal attacks for their alleged neo-colonialist stance, evidenced by their criticism of the budget.[8] The episode illustrates the imprisonment of the West in a system which it created and which

67

it finances. Representatives of the West, even when critical of the United Nations system and of the conduct of its Third World majority, do not contemplate withdrawal or effective resistance, but hope only for improvement. This is Senator Moynihan's position in his much-quoted article 'The US in Opposition', in which he envisages the role of the United States as one of 'loyal opposition' within the United Nations.[9]

4

The International Development Association (IDA) is a major multi-national aid agency. In the 1970s, India and Tanzania were the largest recipients of IDA funds in Asia and Africa respectively.

In the 1970s the government of India waged war against Pakistan, another major IDA recipient; it developed and exploded a nuclear bomb; it engaged in forcible sterilization of many poor people; and it pursued exceedingly wasteful policies of import substitution and other forms of economic control which were much criticized, even by Indian economists sympathetic both to development planning and to foreign aid.

In Tanzania, major government policies in the 1970s included enforced movement of millions of people into villages far from their homes, often involving brutality and hardship. Compulsory collect-ivization of farming was carried out, and there was extensive nationalization of economic activity, expropriation of private property, large-scale persecution of productive groups, and dis-crimination against private enterprises in areas such as transport and trading. These policies had devastating effects on food production and distribution, and on economic conditions generally. They bore harshly on the poorest people. In addition, huge sums were spent on the attempted construction of a brand new capital city. In December 1981 President Nyerere stated publicly that Tanzania was then poorer than ten years earlier.[10] He did not mention his own contribution to this condition. On the contrary, Dr Nyerere has been an articulate exponent of the charge that it is the rich West that has been responsible for the poverty both of his country and of the Third World generally.

Large-scale IDA assistance to Tanzania continued throughout the

68

1970s. Indeed, this aid together with aid from other Western sources was indispensable for Dr Nyerere's political survival. Multinational aid on a large scale continued to flow although, as a World Bank study was to express it, 'Beyond doubt, domestic policies are largely responsible [for] the current economic crisis in Tanzania.'[11]

The story is much the same in Ghana, another recipient of IDA aid, whose economy has for years been characterized by acute shortages of consumer goods and, according to World Bank estimates, has suffered a 3 per cent a year decline in GNP *per capita* between 1970 and 1972.[12] Government policies and incompetent and corrupt administration have been largely responsible for this retrogression.[13]

5

It will be recalled that the Pearson Commission favoured the multinational form of aid also on the ground that the international agencies had an important part to play in the promotion of 'regional integration' among Third World countries. It is hard to take this seriously. There have been numerous conflicts, including armed conflicts, between recipients of multinational aid. The closing of the border between Kenya and Tanzania, both important IDA recipients, has for many years imposed heavy costs on the people of both countries, as well as on others who have been forced to take expensive and circuitous routes in personal travel and for the movement of goods.

Further, it is not at all obvious how the promotion by aid agencies of the policy of regional co-operation can be squared with the notion that it is for each recipient country to choose its own policies and objectives.

6

What provides the momentum behind aid and its increase, and behind multinational aid in particular?

Various interacting forces are at work here, the most important of which are ideology and special interest groups.[14] The ideological forces include feelings of Western guilt towards the Third World, which are intensified by Marxist and neo-Marxist notions; the spread

69

of egalitarianism; and the search for new causes, including the building of a brave new world, fuelled by dissatisfaction in the West with the results of rapid material advance. These ideological forces are apt to thrive unchecked in the context of Western relations with the Third World. Knowledge of conditions in the less developed world inevitably tends to be hazy, and is in any case biased by the sustained flow of news and views emanating from aid organizations and advocates. Aid organizations increasingly devote resources to what is called aid education, that is dissemination of materials which uncritically commend their activities and urge more aid. And some groups have a direct interest in promoting the flow of aid. Notable among these are Western exporters, including their employees and consultants, and the national and international bureaucracies involved in the aid process.

Individual Western governments are apt to favour a shift toward more multinational aid insofar as each expects its own exporters to benefit from Third World purchases financed by multinational aid. Each government expects the value of the additional export orders to exceed its own additional contributions to multinational aid. Additional multinational aid appears to involve little or no net cost to the individual governments. This is especially so when it is financed by methods such as the IMF sales of gold or the issue of its Special Drawing Rights, methods that give the appearance that new resources can be conjured out of thin air.

As a pressure group for more aid, there is, of course, the Third World itself, which for practical purposes is little more than a collective noun for aid-recipient governments. Organized pressure for aid and yet more aid is what unites the Third World, which otherwise consists of widely diverse entities often in conflict with one another. And aid-recipient governments tend to favour multinational aid because their conduct is subject to less control than in principle is exerciseable under national aid (although it is rarely exercised). Further, multinational aid creates even less of a sense of dependence and obligation than does national aid.

The international organizations themselves, delegates and staffs alike, have an evident interest in ever-increasing multinational aid, and are a powerful influence behind its expansion. They provide a platform for Third World governments and spokesmen, as well as

70

advisory and technical machinery and administrative back-up. They have vast resources, some of which are used to influence the donors and to propagate the case for aid and its increase.[15] They are in constant touch with the media and offer patronage, through employment opportunities, to academics and consultants.

We have already noted the influence of the official aid organizations, notably of their permanent staff members. This has contributed greatly to the unquestioning acceptance in the West of the case for wealth transfers and their increase. It may also, for example, help to explain the frequent expressions of apprehension in the West that governments of ldcs might refuse to accept aid if the Western donors criticized their domestic or foreign policies, or objected to the insults meted out to the donors by aid recipients. The implementation of such a threat would, of course, benefit taxpayers in the donor countries, but would damage the interests of the aid administrators whose activities it would diminish.

7

Further expansion of multinational aid is probable. The effective interest groups ranged behind it have been considered in the preceding section. Moreover, since the 1960s the emphasis in aid advocacy has been shifting in directions that favour multinational aid.

There is now more emphasis than before on the notion that aid is a global co-operative activity in which donors and recipients must participate. The Pearson Report of 1969, with its major theme of more aid, notably multinational aid, has the title *Partners in Development*. The Brandt Report of 1980 speaks of global survival, and of aid and the international organizations as its indispensable instruments.

In recent years aid has increasingly come to be canvassed as an instrument for the international redistribution of income. The 1974 United Nations Declaration of the New International Economic Order was the major landmark in this particular shift of emphasis. If aid is to serve as an instrument of systematic worldwide redistribution, it would have to be multinational and centrally organized.

There are few signs in the West of effective resistance to the expansion of multinational aid. Divisions in the West undermine

71

what resistance there might be, divisions which might reflect ideological differences or differences in perceived political and economic interests. I have already noted an example of such divisions in the context of the FAO budget conference of 1981.

Another example is provided by a recent event within the IMF, usually regarded as a citadel of the West. At its meeting held in Gabon in May 1981, the five major contributors of aid to the Third World, which between them provided over 75 per cent of all Western aid, jointly proposed Sir Geoffrey Howe, the British Chancellor of the Exchequer, as chairman of an influential IMF committee. They failed. His election was blocked by Third World representatives, supported by some Western delegates. The Third World representatives objected to the British Government's alleged lack of understanding of Third World problems. At the time, British aid was about £1 billion a year.[16]

The Third World position in this case was widely seen in press comments as appropriate on the ground that Third World countries should participate in the administration of the IMF and of other aid organizations generally because these countries were their clients or customers. The bizarre nature of this argument is evident. It is like saying that banks should be run by their borrowers, or charities by their beneficiaries. Banks and charities would soon have to terminate their activities if they were so administered. The self-correcting mechanism of bankruptcy is not present in the operation of official aid organizations, as these can draw on taxpayers for replenishment of their resources.

CHAPTER 5

Ecclesiastical Economics: Envy Legitimized

After Pryde wol I speken of the foule sinne of Envye, which is, as by the word of the philosophre, sorwe [sorrow] *of other mannes prosperitee.*

Chaucer, *The Parson's Tale*

1

Envy is traditionally one of the seven deadly sins. Vocal modern clerical opinion endows it with moral legitimacy and intellectual respectability. The results of this specious legitimization of envy are the principal themes of this chapter.

2

Since the Second World War, prominent clergymen and theologians have been much preoccupied with domestic and international differences in income and wealth. A broad consensus has emerged, and its supporters range from recent popes to explicitly Marxist clerics.

The following are the central theme and its supporting arguments. Social justice requires that incomes should be substantially equal; appreciable differences in incomes reflect exploitation, oppression, discrimination or improper privilege; and politically organized redistribution is desirable, or even a Christian duty. These opinions are particularly common, insistent and strident in discussions on economic differences between the West and the Third World, and on those within individual Third World countries.

I shall discuss these opinions primarily by examining two influential documents by Pope Paul VI: the Encyclical Letter, *Populorum Progressio* (1967), and the Pontifical Letter, *Octogesima Adveniens* (1971), referred to hereafter as the papal documents or letters. The two documents must be treated synoptically as the latter relies

73

heavily on the former, which is also generally more explicit than its successor.[1]

3

The main theme of the papal documents is that economic differences, consistently termed inequalities, reflect injustice.

According to these papal documents, substantial economic differences reflect the perversion of that just and natural state which is to be expected from the fact that God has created the earth for all mankind and created man in his image. The differences result from the exploitation and oppression of the weak by the strong, including denial of opportunities to the former by the latter.

The Pope quotes the Second Vatican Council: 'God intended the earth and all that it contains for the use of every human being and people' (*Populorum Progressio* 22). He then quotes St Ambrose: 'You are not making a gift of your possessions to the poor person. You are handing over to him what is his. For what has been given in common for the use of all, you have arrogated to yourself. The world is given to all, and not only to the rich' (*Populorum Progressio* 23).

These passages are reproduced on posters and in leaflets in numerous churches in the West. Often they refer particularly to the Third World, usually in terms such as that the earth belongs to all its peoples, yet at the same time three-quarters of them do not share in it.

Subsidiary themes support the main theme, that inequality means injustice. A major problem is the question of '. . . the fairness in the exchange of goods and in the division of wealth between individuals and countries' (*Octogesima Adveniens* 7). The economic system left to itself widens international economic differences: '. . . rich peoples enjoy rapid growth whereas the poor develop slowly. The imbalance is on the increase: some produce a surplus of foodstuffs, others cruelly lack them and see their exports made uncertain' (*Populorum Progressio* 8).

Again, 'in trade between developed and underdeveloped economies, conditions are too disparate and the degrees of genuine freedom available too unequal' (*Populorum Progressio* 61). This inequality is responsible for the persistent deterioration in the terms of trade of primary producers. 'The value of manufactured goods is rapidly increasing and they can always find an adequate market. On the other hand, raw materials produced by underdeveloped countries are subject to wide and sudden fluctuations in price, a state of affairs far removed from the progressively increasing value of industrial products. . . . The poor nations remain ever poor while the rich ones become still richer' (*Populorum Progressio* 57).

In some cases the difficulties are legacies of colonialism. The colonial rulers have sometimes 'left a precarious economy bound up for instance with the production of one kind of crop whose market prices are subject to sudden and considerable variation' (*Populorum Progressio* 7).

The situation calls for urgent action: 'We must make haste: too many are suffering and the distance is growing that separates the progress of some and the stagnation, not to say the regression, of others' (*Populorum Progressio* 29).

Both within countries and also on the international plane, inequalities of wealth go hand in hand with inequalities of power: 'There is also the scandal of glaring inequalities not merely in the enjoyment of possessions but even more in the exercise of power. While a small restricted group enjoys a refined civilization in certain regions, the remainder of the population, poor and scattered, is deprived of nearly all possibility of personal initiative and of responsibility, and often times even its living and working conditions are unworthy of the human person' (*Populorum Progressio* 9).

The Pope refers also to '. . . unproductive monopolization of resources by a small number of men' (*Populorum Progressio* 66). All these differences lead to '. . . social conflicts which have taken on world dimensions' (*Populorum Progressio* 9).

Specific groups are singled out for condemnation. They include landowners whose 'landed estates impede the general prosperity because they are extensive, unused or poorly used, or because they bring hardship to peoples or are detrimental to the interests of the country (so that the common good sometimes demands their expropriation)' (*Populorum Progressio* 24). There are also people who transfer part of their money '. . . abroad purely for their own advantage, without care for the manifest wrong they inflict on their country by doing this' (*ibid.*).

There are those who create superfluous wants, so that while '. . . very large numbers of people are unable to satisfy their primary needs, superfluous needs are ingeniously created' (*Octogesima Adveniens* 9). There are those who derive 'inadmissible profits' through speculation in necessities (*Octogesima Adveniens* 10). Leaders of multinational enterprises are chided for returning to '. . . inhuman principles of individualism when they operate in less developed countries' (*Populorum Progressio* 70).

There are also specific categories of victims of injustice. These include people who cannot find '. . . a decent dwelling at a price they can afford' (*Octogesima Adveniens* 11); and those '. . . who are denied the right to work [at] equitable remuneration' (*Octogesima Adveniens* 14).

Suggestions or hints for action are scattered about in the two documents. The suggestions are often extremely vague, and at times implicit rather than explicit. However, the general direction is clear. It is along the following lines.

Christians must do their best in a spirit of charity to remedy the injustice of social, cultural and especially economic differences, which, according to the Pope, at times cries to heaven. Individual action is insufficient to deal with the problems. Collective action is required and to be effective has to be political. This is so partly because of the magnitude of the problems. Another even more important reason why action has to be collective and political is that, in the explicit opinion of the Pope, governments always act for the common good (*Octogesima Adveniens* 46, quoted below). The efforts should take the form primarily of concerted international actions and plans.

The proposals revolve around the theme of politically organized redistribution. The primary theme is the urgent need for official international wealth transfers to redress existing international inequality and injustice and thereby to promote development and peace.

These official transfers are necessary '. . . to further the progress of poorer peoples, to encourage social justice among nations, to offer to less developed nations the means whereby they can further their own progress' (*Populorum Progressio* 5). For this purpose 'all available resources should be pooled' (*Populorum Progressio* 43).

'Advanced nations have a very heavy obligation to help the

developing peoples. . . . Every nation must produce more and better quality goods to give to all its inhabitants a truly human standard of living, and also to contribute to the common development of the human race' (*Populorum Progressio* 48).

'We must repeat once more that the superfluous wealth of rich countries should be placed at the service of poor nations. The rule which up to now held good for the benefit of those nearest to us, must today be applied to all the needy of this world. Besides, the rich will be the first to benefit as a result. Otherwise their continued greed will certainly call down upon them the judgement of God and the wrath of the poor, with consequences no one can foretell' (*Populorum Progressio* 49).

'May everyone be convinced of this: the very life of poor nations, civil peace in developing countries, and world peace itself are at stake' (*Populorum Progressio* 55).

In international trade, major changes are required to rectify the inequality of bargaining power between the West and the Third World and the lack of genuine economic freedom of the latter. International agreements '. . . would establish general norms for regulating certain prices, for guaranteeing certain types of production, for supporting certain new industries' (*Populorum Progressio* 61). 'Internationally organized investment, production, trade and education would help to create employment in countries where population is growing rapidly' (*Octogesima Adveniens* 18).

Other suggestions for international action include technical assistance to less developed countries, and regional agreements among weak nations for mutual support (*Populorum Progressio* 71, 77).

The Pope writes under the heading 'Development is the New Name for Peace': 'Excessive economic, social and cultural inequalities among peoples arouse tensions and conflicts, and are a danger to peace. . . . To wage war on misery and to struggle against injustice is to promote, along with improved conditions, the human and spiritual progress of all men, and therefore the common good of humanity. Peace cannot be limited to a mere absence of war' (*Populorum Progressio* 76).

The United Nations has a key role 'to bring not some people but all peoples to treat each other as brothers. . . . Who does not see the necessity of thus establishing progressively a world authority capable of acting effectively in the juridical and political sectors?' (*Populorum Progressio* 78). 'Some would consider such hopes Utopian. It may be . . . that they have not perceived the dynamism of the world which desires to live more fraternally' (*Populorum Progressio* 79).

The Pope also envisages far-reaching policies within countries to promote progress and to remedy injustice: 'Development demands bold transformations, innovations that go deep. Urgent reforms should be undertaken without delay' (*Populorum Progressio* 32). 'As we have seen, these reforms will include expropriation of the properties of at least some categories of landowners' (*Populorum Progressio* 24).

Under the heading 'Programmes and Planning' the Pope writes: 'It pertains to the public authorities to choose, even to lay down, the objectives to be pursued in economic development, the ends to be achieved, and the means of attaining them, and it is for them to stimulate all the forces engaged in this common activity' (*Populorum Progressio* 33). These tasks must be left to governments, to the representatives of political power, '. . . which is the natural and necessary link for ensuring the cohesion of the social body. . . . It always intervenes with careful justice and with devotion to the common good for which it holds final responsibility' (*Octogesima Adveniens* 46).

The ultimate aim is to build a world where 'every man, no matter what his race, religion or nationality, can live a full human life, freed from servitude imposed upon him by other men or by natural forces over which he has not sufficient control; a world where freedom is not an empty word and where the poor man Lazarus can sit down at the same table with the rich man' (*Populorum Progressio* 47).

4

The Pope's diagnosis and proposals are remarkably commonplace. There is nothing distinctively Christian or Catholic about them. They were already in vogue when the pronouncements were issued, and they are still in vogue today.[2] They are to be found, for example, in so secular a document as the Brandt report, *North–South: A Pro-*

gramme for Survival.

Third World Catholic opinions on these matters are particularly notable because by the end of the century the great majority of Catholics are likely to be in the Third World, primarily Latin America. Here are some examples, which again I shall quote without at this point examining their validity.

According to Monsenor Alfonso Lopez Trujillo, the Secretary General of the Latin American Bishops' Conference: 'The United States and Canada are rich because the peoples of Latin America are poor. They have built their wealth on top of us.'[3]

Dom Helder Camara, known as Brother of the Poor or the Red Bishop, has become an international figure with speaking engagements all over the world. In an interview with the London-based magazine *South* (December 1980) headed 'The Church that Refuses to Think for the Poor', he is reported as saying:

But it [rural poverty] is not a local problem: it is a national problem, even a continental problem. You know that the prices of our raw materials have always been set in the great decision-making centres of the world. . . . And while we [the Catholic Church] supported what amounted to social disorder, the United Nations were proclaiming that two-thirds of mankind live in inhuman conditions of misery and hunger.

Dr Julius Nyerere, President of Tanzania (and a Catholic), said in London a few years ago:

In one world, as in one state, when I am rich because you are poor, and I am poor because you are rich, the transfer of wealth from the rich to the poor is a matter of right; it is not an appropriate matter for charity. . . . If the rich nations go on getting richer and richer at the expense of the poor, the poor of the world must demand a change in the same way as the proletariat in the rich countries demanded a change in the past.[4]

Finally, an example from an influential source which explicitly brings in the multinational companies. Peter Nichols, Rome correspondent of *The Times* (London), wrote in his much-publicized book *The Pope's Divisions* (London 1981): 'Much of the economy [of Latin America] is dominated by multinationals who take out basic raw materials in return for impossible wages'.[5]

79

5

Income differences cannot be discussed sensibly without looking at their background. Individuals, groups and societies can be poor for any number of different reasons. Thus a person may become poor because he has habitually overspent a large income; or he may be poor for circumstances entirely beyond his control such as incurable disease, confiscation of his assets, or the restriction of his opportunities. Individuals and groups may be materially unambitious. Contrast for instance the conduct and position of Malays and Chinese in Malaysia. Again, if many poor people survive longer in an ldc, this depresses *per capita* incomes and leads to what is habitually termed a worsening of income distribution, both within the particular country and relative to richer countries. Conversely, if more of the poor die or a society reverts to subsistence production, this brings about more equal incomes within a country, accompanied by a rise in *per capita* incomes in the former case and a decline in the latter case.

In egalitarian discourse, the notion that the well-off have prospered at the expense of the poor is rarely far below the surface, a notion which is useful or even necessary for the moral plausibility of politically organized redistribution. Without such an underpinning, the case for redistributive taxation (which in effect is partial confiscation) or for other forms of expropriation is not self-evident. Why should social justice mean substantially equal incomes? Why is it obviously unjust that those who contribute more to production should have higher incomes than those who contribute less?

The case for politically organized redistribution becomes yet more dubious when it is remembered that this policy is apt to aggravate the lot of the poorest as well as to aggrandize those who organize the transfers. To begin with, state-organized redistribution often benefits middle income groups at the expense both of the rich and of the poor. This is now widely recognized in the context of redistribution within a country, especially when the benefits accruing to the administrators of these policies are also taken into account. Moreover, redistribution inhibits enterprise and effort and the accumulation and productive deployment of capital, and this result retards a rise in living standards, including those of the poorest.

The adverse effects of redistribution on the living standards of the poorest are perforce ignored when income and wealth are envisaged, as they often are, as being extracted from other people, or somehow achieved at their expense by depriving them of what they had or could have had. They are regarded as fixed totals rather than as the results of productive activities and processes over time. In market economies, however, incomes are normally earned; they are not shares in a pre-existing total.

Group differences in economic performance abound in the Third World. In Malaysia, for instance, Chinese economic performance has for many years been far superior to that of Malays in spite of long-standing discrimination against them. In recent years, indeed, attempts to combat by political means the results of their superior economic performance have become the cornerstone of official economic policy. (Other examples of the relative success of groups discriminated against are commonplace in economic history.) In Latin America also, the prosperity of the landowners, industrialists and merchants has not been achieved at the expense of the poor. The economic conditions of the poorest groups, such as the Indians of Central and Southern America and the Negro descendants of slaves in Brazil, are no worse, and in many ways are far better, than were those of their ancestors. The economic conditions of Negroes in Brazil do not differ greatly from those of Africans in the more advanced parts of black Africa.

The notion that the incomes of the more prosperous have somehow been achieved at the expense of the less prosperous has had a long and disastrous history. In its duration and consequences it is perhaps the most pernicious of all economic misconceptions. On the contemporary scene it has contributed to the persecution of economically productive but politically unpopular and powerless minorities in the Third World.

There are, of course, major exceptions to the general proposition that the incomes of the prosperous are earned. Perhaps the most important exceptions are incomes derived predominantly from government-conferred privileges. Such privileges are especially significant and widespread in the extremely politicized societies of the Third World. Their many forms include state subsidies, restrictions on competition, allocations of licences and privileged forms of employment. These privileged incomes are not what the Pope and other clerics have in mind in their attacks on inequality. Such

81

privileged incomes are not relevant to international differences in income. And in the national sphere it is the papal view that governments act for the general good, so that the results of their policies cannot be the subject for redress through politically organized redistribution. Moreover, recipients of such privileged incomes are not necessarily rich. Finally, egalitarian discourse is addressed to income differences as such, not to privileged incomes *vis-à-vis* other incomes.[6]

6

Sometimes the papal documents do not ascribe the poverty of the poor to exploitation or oppression. Instead, the failure of poor people, notably poor societies, to share in contemporary prosperity is attributed to lack of natural resources, especially land.

Lack of natural resources, including land, has little or nothing to do with the poverty of individuals or of societies. Amidst abundant land and natural resources the Indians before Columbus remained wretchedly poor when much of Europe with far less land was already rich. In the less developed world today, many millions of extremely poor people have abundant cultivable land. Over much of Asia, Africa and Latin America very large numbers of extremely poor and backward people live in areas where cultivable but uncultivated land is free or extremely cheap. The small size and low productivity of farms and the presence of landless workers in such areas reflect not the shortage of land but primarily the lack of ambition, enterprise and skill.

Of course, land which has been improved by the efforts and savings of productive people is the target for demands for redistribution even where unimproved land is plentiful. Who would not welcome a free gift of valuable assets? Land on its own is unproductive, and yields nothing of value to mankind. It becomes productive as a result of ambition, perceptiveness, resourcefulness and effort. These attributes and characteristics are present very unequally among different individuals, groups and societies.

Sustained prosperity, as distinct from occasional windfalls, owes little or nothing to natural resources: witness West Germany, Switzerland, Japan, Singapore, Hong Kong and Taiwan. The wide differences in economic performance between individuals and groups in the same country with access to the same natural resources throw into relief the personal and cultural differences behind economic achievement.

The conditions of the poorest and most backward people throughout the Third World, such as tribal societies, pygmies and aborigines, cannot possibly have anything to do with lack of land, Western exploitation or the activities of ethnic minorities.

These groups have few contacts either with the West or with economically active ethnic minorities. They also have abundant land at their disposal. Much the same applies to the causes of famine and to the lack of so-called basic facilities. For instance, the famines in sparsely populated African countries such as Ethiopia, the Sahel, Tanzania, Uganda and Zaire reflect the low level of subsistence or near-subsistence activity, perpetuated or aggravated by the lack of public security and by damaging policies such as official suppression of trading activity, forced collectivization and the persecution of productive groups, notably ethnic or tribal minorities.

7

Domestic and international redistribution are the overriding policy prescriptions in the papal documents. The former is to be effected by taxation or outright confiscation; the latter by politically organized government-to-government transfers of resources, known as foreign aid. I have questioned the case for domestic redistribution in section 5 above.[7] The economic, political, social and moral implications of foreign aid are the subject of Chapter 3 in this volume, and there is no need to traverse the same ground here. It is evident from Chapter 3 that the papal documents ignore all the major issues involved in attempted global redistribution by means of foreign aid given to governments on the basis of the poverty of their subjects.

I turn now to some issues, including moral issues, raised by the Pope's general approach to income differences and to the policies appropriate to their reduction or elimination. This approach entails major spiritual and moral implications and consequences which many people may well consider even more destructive than the political and economic effects. I should perhaps recall here that the Pope's

83

opinions expressed in *Populorum Progressio* and *Octogesima Adveniens* reflect what is virtually a consensus of opinions of contemporary churchmen on what they call social justice. Indeed, the language of the younger Catholic clergy and of Protestant churchmen is apt to be much more strident.

The persistent preoccupation with income differences and with the contrast in prosperity between the West and the Third World is much more likely to arouse envy than to elicit compassion. The allegations that prosperity reflects misconduct and therefore injustice lace envy with resentment and righteous indignation. Such notions also reflect and reinforce the contemporary tendency to play down personal responsibility by suggesting that people's economic conditions depend on external forces rather than on themselves.

The modern clerical consensus endorsed by the Pope buttresses and encourages envy and resentment by conferring apparent moral legitimacy and intellectual validity on these sentiments. Insistence on politically organized redistribution within and between countries also fuels envy and resentment. Articulate clergymen and many academics have traditionally shared an attitude of suspicion and hostility towards people actively engaged in the process of wealth creation, and also an attitude of supercilious disdain for its results.

Envy and resentment are soul-destroying sentiments liable to corrode people afflicted by them. What the Pope asserts, in common with so many other modern clergymen, serves to encourage one of the seven deadly sins.

To arouse these sentiments is to provoke tension and conflict. In this way conflicts originating in politicization or in other influences can be extended, intensified and brutalized. Moreover, the fear of being exposed to envy and to its political and social consequences inhibits economic performance and improvement. This applies notably in tribal societies.

The catch-phrase 'the earth belongs to all' epitomizes the central thrust of the papal documents and is bound to provoke envy, or something stronger. This slogan has become a rallying cry in inflammatory propaganda against the West and against well-to-do people both in the Third World and in the West. The principal theme is that some three-quarters of mankind languish in poverty, excluded from their rightful heritage through misconduct of the well-to-do,

84

and especially by the sinister domination of Western financial institutions and multinational companies.

A leaflet distributed in Chartres cathedral in 1979 is typical. Entitled (not surprisingly) 'The Earth Belongs to All' ('*La terre est à tous*'), the leaflet quotes a resolution of thirteen Brazilian bishops – who claim to be the voice of their voiceless people – that nothing will change in their country without fundamental changes in the advanced countries where the centres of domination and private capital are located. The leaflet insists that radical changes in the West are necessary to bring about a new international economic order, meaning large-scale confiscation of wealth as restitution for supposed economic wrongs. These political demands are described as the essence of Christ's message – the only mention of Christ in the four-page document.

Such propaganda plays upon and reinforces the widespread feeling of guilt in the West towards the Third World, a feeling which does nothing to assist the ordinary people in ldcs, but is more likely to harm them.[8] Exponents of collective guilt rarely examine either the ground for their allegations or the results of the policies they propose. In the context of foreign aid, such allegations are most likely to lead to indiscriminate wealth transfers to Third World governments and to various international organizations. The emphasis on guilt precludes close examination either of conditions in the recipient countries or of the conduct of the recipient governments. These considerations are pertinent, especially because guilt so often parades as compassion and is so readily confused with it. The exponents of guilt routinely exempt themselves from their accusations; they do not speak of *mea culpa* but of *nostra culpa*, or rather *vestra culpa*. This is not accidental; allegations of collective guilt go hand in hand with a decline in personal responsibility and a sense of personal sin.

The Pope regards official transfers as a discharge of moral duty and as action substantially similar to voluntary charity. Yet there is an evident difference in moral content between voluntary sacrifice to help one's fellow men and public spending out of taxes. Taxpayers have no choice, and many may not know that they contribute for this particular purpose. The political and economic effects of the two forms of transfer also differ profoundly. The activities of voluntary agencies, especially non-politicized charities, do not politicize life as

85

does official foreign aid, and thus they avoid the baleful results of the politicization of life promoted by official transfers. Moreover, voluntary charity is generally adjusted far more effectively to the conditions and needs of local people. In particular, voluntary agencies are much more interested in alleviating the lot of the poorest than are most rulers in the Third World.

At one point the Pope insists on liberating people from subjection to the forces of nature. But many millions of people in Asia do not share the Western outlook that nature should be harnessed to man's purposes. They think or feel that man should learn to live with nature rather than try to subordinate it to his own purposes. Generally, Western culture envisages nature as serving the purpose of man, who has the right, indeed the duty, to subordinate it to his own purposes. The indigenous cultures of South Asia envisage organic creation as a continuum which man has no special right to subject to his own purposes.

The Pope enjoins his audience to respect non-Western civilizations and cultures. The cultures of large parts of the less developed world are uncongenial to economic achievement and advance. The idea of material progress, in the sense of a steadily increasing control by man over nature, is wholly of Western origin. It is anomalous to insist that the West should respect Third World cultures and at the same time to urge that the West should pay taxes for the benefit of those who embrace cultures inimical to economic advance.

In the face of the clerical consensus on Western responsibility for Third World poverty, it was unexpected and refreshing recently to find an opinion by a Third World prelate who disagrees fundamentally with received opinion and who has the moral courage to say so. He is Monseigneur Bernard Bududira, Bishop of Bururi in Burundi in Central Africa, and an African. Part of an article by the Bishop in a French-language African journal was reproduced in German translation in the Swiss newspaper *Neue Zürcher Zeitung* of 4/5 January 1981. It is a remarkable article.

Bishop Bududira's principal theme is that the local cultures in Africa and elsewhere in the Third World obstruct material progress. The Bishop insists that economic improvement of a person depends on the person himself, notably on his mental attitudes and especially on his attitude to work. Unquestioning acceptance of nature and of its

86

vagaries is widespread in Africa and elsewhere in the Third World. Man sees himself not as making history but as suffering it. To regard life as inexorably ordained by fate prevents a person from developing his or her potential. Under these influences people become passive rather than active, and the obligations of the extended family system stifle ambition and creative imagination. Initiative may be inhibited further by dependence upon tribal groups which suppress innovation and regard efforts for change and improvement as forms of rebellion. The Bishop concludes that the message of Christ frees people from the shackles of tribal thinking, and leads to a greater sense of personal responsibility. The required changes can best be achieved by Christian groups working with local communities.

Some of these ideas used to be familiar, but they are very rarely heard nowadays. The translator commented that only an African could now write such an article. This observation is notable recognition of the success of the pedlars of Western guilt. Were it not for this factor, it would be by no means obvious why a European should not now write along such lines.

8

According to the opening paragraph of *Populorum Progressio*, the document is to help people 'to grasp their serious problems in all its dimensions . . . at this turning point in human history'. This promise is not fulfilled. The papal letters are not theological, doctrinal or philosophical statements reaffirming Christian beliefs or helping people to find their bearings. They are political statements supported by bogus arguments, and as such can only confuse believers.

As will be clear from what has gone before, the Pope has lost all contact with reality, both in what he says and what he ignores. Amidst large-scale civil conflict (as in Nigeria and Vietnam at the time of *Populorum Progressio*), massacres, mass persecution and expulsions in ldcs, the Pope wrote about the solidarity and brotherhood of humanity in the less developed world, and also stated that governments always act for the common good. He ignores the relation between culture and economic achievement and the relevance of mores and beliefs to economic performance and progress. There is also a complete disregard of historical processes and of the perspective of time, as evidenced by the neglect of the fact that until very recently extreme material backwardness characterized most of the Third World. And yet applications of the time perspective used to be very much an element in Catholic thinking.

Even the eternal verities are overlooked. The responsibility of a person for the consequences of his actions and the fundamental distinction between mankind and the rest of creation are basic Christian tenets. They are pertinent to the issues raised by the Pope; but they are ignored throughout these documents.

In common with many other modern Christian clerics, Paul vi, his predecessor John xxiii, and to some extent also John Paul ii, have chosen to speak on subjects with which they have been unfamiliar. People who pronounce on matters about which they are ignorant are apt simply to absorb ideas propagated or taken up by other élite or establishment groups. Nature abhors a vacuum not only in the physical world but also in the world of politics and ideas.

The Pope's arguments and allegations reflect unthinking surrender to intellectual fashion and political nostrums. This is obvious in the major themes, particularly in the insistence on large-scale official aid. The more specific topics and proposals are also a recital of modish remedies such as land reform, debt cancellation, commodity agreements and regional co-operation among ldcs.

The spirit of these documents is contrary to the most durable and best elements in Catholic tradition. They are indeed even un-Christian. Their Utopian, chiliastic ideology, combined with an overriding preoccupation with economic differences, is an amalgam of the ideas of millenarian sects, of the extravagant claims of the early American advocates of foreign aid, and of the Messianic component of Marxism-Leninism.

There is a familiar and ominous ring in the insistence that economic advance requires 'bold transformations, innovations that go deep' by political means. Such a stance has been regularly advanced to justify pervasive coercion and brutal policies. These harsh consequences are a familiar outcome of replacing conduct based on experience and reflection by ideological politics. In this sphere also it is true that those who wish to turn men into angels are more likely to turn them into beasts. The chiliasm of these documents is alien to the traditional down-to-earth attitude of the Catholic Church in worldly matters.

88

Populorum Progressio and *Octogesima Adveniens* are documents which are immoral on several levels. To begin with they are incompetent, and they are immoral because they are incompetent. Their lack of reflection and ideological commitment leads to proposals and promotes policies directly at variance with the declared sentiments and objectives of the papal documents. There is profound truth in Pascal's maxim that working hard to think clearly is the beginning of moral conduct. This applies with altogether special force to the head of a worldwide Church issuing major pronouncements. The documents are also immoral in that they give colour to the notion that envy can be legitimate; and they spread confusion about the meaning of charity.

It seems that many contemporary churchmen have lost their way and have moved into realms which are strange to them. They may perhaps have been seeking a new role for themselves in the face of widespread erosion or even the collapse of traditional beliefs. Their preoccupations may reflect a panic reaction to fear of the loss of their clientele. Some of the utterances of the modern clergy recall Othello's predicament when he felt that his occupation had gone, together with the attendant pomp and circumstance. It is paradoxical that the clergy are preoccupied with material conditions and progress at a time when the failure of material prosperity and advance to secure happiness, satisfaction and tranquillity is everywhere evident.

Acceptance of ideas plainly at variance with reality may, however, also reflect the ready credulity of people, clerics included, who have lost their faith. Chesterton predicted long ago that when men cease to believe in a deity, they do not believe in nothing: they then simply believe in anything.

Truth may be great and will perhaps prevail. Scholars at any rate must act as if they believed both parts of this statement. But it requires exceptional strength of belief to hope that truth will triumph in the decades ahead in egalitarian discussions, especially about the Third World. The modern clerical consensus will certainly not help it to victory. Prelates such as Bishop Bududira might do so.

CHAPTER 6

Black Africa: the Living Legacy of Dying Colonialism

1

There is a stereotype of the historical experience of British colonial Africa which holds that these territories stagnated or even retrogressed during most of the colonial era as a result of administrative neglect and commercial exploitation. According to the same stereotype, the rulers mended their ways somewhat in the terminal phase of colonialism and concerned themselves more actively with the welfare of their subjects.

Both parts of this stereotype are very nearly the opposite of the truth. British colonial rule before the 1930s benefited the great majority of Africans. But it offered little scope for the political ambitions of the limited groups who were later to come into prominence, and to form the political nation. These Africans benefited greatly, at the expense of the inarticulate and politically ineffective majority, from the policies introduced in the closing period of colonialism.

2

In British Africa, as elsewhere, colonial conquest had often been accompanied by bloodshed, and early colonial rule frequently involved the levy of forced labour.[1] This phase was largely over by the end of the nineteenth century, and by the late nineteenth and early twentieth centuries, British colonial administrations governed firmly but lightly. They did not attempt to control closely the lives and activities of their subjects. Taxation was modest and people enjoyed virtually complete personal freedom, including the freedom to choose their own activities, to move around the country unheeded, and to dispose of their incomes as they wished. Tribal warfare, slavery and slavetrading – formerly widespread or endemic – had been effectively suppressed.

The most important guiding principles of administration were those of limited government (including limited intervention in economic life); reliance on local institutions as far as possible; acceptance of traditional leaders and local councils as the representatives of African opinion and interests; and gradual evolution and reform of traditional authorities in preparation for independence. These principles were epitomized by Joyce Cary in his reminiscences of his life in the colonial service in Nigeria:

It was the rule then in the Nigerian Service, and has always been one of the guiding principles of British colonial policy, to preserve local law and custom as far as possible, and to do nothing that might break the continuity of local government. Tribal chiefs and tribal councils were to be maintained, and progress made by educating chiefs, by improving their roads, public services – which (as experience shows) by itself modifies the whole situation and can (if that end is kept in view) quite quickly build up a class capable of some share in the government, on the first elementary representative committees. . . .

But the first principle was absolute: Do not break the continuity. Do not attempt to force a constitution on the people. However good it may seem, however suitable to the place and time (and this is granting a lot), it will be hated and sabotaged. So it will serve only as a bar to all constitutional development. . . .

The essential points of emphasis in our administration were continuity and balance. We were not to destroy native rule and economic custom, but to develop them on their own roots. . . .[2]

British colonial government was readily accepted because it followed these principles, and this in turn made government relatively easy and inexpensive.

The accepted guidelines of colonial policies by no means implied governmental inactivity, but required the effective performance of traditional and necessary functions. These functions included protection against external aggression; the establishment and maintenance of public security (which encompassed suppression of slavery and slavetrading and also of tribal warfare); the effective management of the monetary and fiscal systems; construction and maintenance of transport facilities; provision of some basic educational, public health and veterinary services; and some agricultural extension work.

In West Africa, efficient performance of these tasks helped to promote the spread of the growth of cash crops for export and for domestic use, while the growth of a large volume of imports provided incentives for improved economic performance. Between the 1880s and the 1930s, conditions of existence were transformed over large areas, primarily through the emergence and spread of crops such as groundnuts, palm oil, palm kernels, coffee, cotton, kola nuts and cocoa.

In his book *The Economic Revolution in British West Africa* (1926), Alan McPhee, economic historian of West Africa, wrote that the changes brought about by the rise of the cocoa industry represented the superimposition of the twentieth century AD on the twentieth century BC. This extensive transformation took place relatively smoothly. People were not much concerned as to who was in power, so long as government maintained public security and facilitated individual endeavour but did not impinge directly on their personal activities, or obviously and directly affect their livelihood, or abruptly dislocate their established ways. The early colonial administrations respected the traditions of different societies, and people voluntarily adjusted to newly emerging economic opportunities.

In these conditions, Dr Johnson's dictum fully applied, that 'Public affairs vex no man'. Ordinary Africans, like ordinary people the world over, are more interested in not being misgoverned than they are in constitutional forms. Firm but limited government which addressed itself to the primary tasks was therefore agreeable to the population at large, a fact rarely acknowledged by African politicians.[3]

3

Between the 1930s and 1950s, the interrelated guiding principles, which had been widely regarded as almost axiomatic, were totally reversed. The process was well under way by 1940, gained momentum in the 1940s and 1950s, and was complete by the end of colonial rule. One system had been superseded by its exact opposite.

The idea that gradual political and social evolution should take place before independence was replaced by insistence on the early introduction of Westminster-style democracy, interpreted as universal suffrage, a system alien to British Africa. The prospective heirs of British rule were no longer the traditional rulers and councils, but articulate Westernized groups, mostly people in contact with their opposite numbers in Britain. Limited government intervention in economic affairs was supplanted (except in subsistence farming) by an increasing preoccupation with detailed and comprehensive economic controls. At the same time, the British colonial administrators neglected basic functions of government, including even the maintenance of public security.[4]

The abrupt overthrow of the main pillars of pre-war colonial policy was by no means welcomed by ordinary Africans. Some candid observations by a prominent Nigerian politician of the early post-war years are instructive:

> Given a choice from among white officials, Chiefs and educated Nigerians as the principal rulers of the country, the illiterate man today would exercise his preference for the three in the order in which they are named. He is convinced, *and he has good reasons to be*, that he can always get better treatment from the white man than he could hope to get from the Chiefs and the educated elements.[5]

The new men brought to the fore by the abrupt change of policy of the late colonial period were largely urban groups, articulate, Westernized politicians, and their allies in the military, in the professions and in business. Many of them, including the educated, had little respect for the rural population and its ways, and were therefore apt to look down on the great majority of their countrymen.

It was not inevitable that this particular class should succeed the colonial rulers. It was certainly not inevitable that the new rulers should be handed a system of close economic controls which placed the bulk of the population at their mercy. The controls need never have been established, or, failing that, could have been dismantled before the end of colonial rule. Their introduction was particularly significant, for without it the other changes might not have had such durable, pervasive, and often violent repercussions.[6]

By the end of the colonial period, an extensive range of economic controls operated in British Africa. Indeed, most of the types of control cited in Chapter 2, section 9, were being employed. The operation of the state export monopolies and the control of imports are examined in some detail in later sections because of their far-reaching effects.

The incoming African rulers welcomed the various controls because they gave them a close grip over their subjects, and enabled them to pursue more effectively their personal and political purposes. They extended these controls whenever they could.

4

In the 1930s, belief in the efficacy of state action for the solution of economic problems, and a corresponding distrust of market forces, had gained ground rapidly in Britain and elsewhere. These ideas were strongly held and propounded by influential civil servants in the Colonial Office and the Colonial Service during the period from the eve of the Second World War until decolonization. The group included Sir Andrew Cohen, who was head of the African Department of the Colonial Office; Sir Jock McPherson (Lord McPherson), who became Governor of Nigeria and eventually head of the Colonial Office; and Sir Hugh Foot (Lord Caradon), who was Chief Secretary of Nigeria. Several of them took for granted the case for the most diverse forms of state economic intervention, including the restrictive licensing of trade. They tended also to support the Westernized African intellectuals rather than the traditional local rulers and authorities.

This so-called 'progressive' group was fortunate in its political leaders. Some of the Secretaries of State for the Colonies over this period were ready to accept the proposals of their most articulate officials, especially if these accorded with widely prevailing ideas. For different reasons, two of the more active Secretaries of State – Arthur Creech Jones (a dedicated Fabian socialist) and Oliver Lyttelton (Lord Chandos) – sympathized with the dirigiste group. Lyttelton, under whose régime state export monopolies were finally imposed on the unfortunate farmers, was a Conservative whose political career was sandwiched between two spells in private business. He was an uncritical supporter of large-scale investment spending, both public and private, and was unsympathetic to small-scale economic activities including small-scale farming.

The centralization of decision-making in the Colonial Office and in the Secretariats, and the diminution of the powers of governors and district officers, promoted the diffusion of controls in the late colonial period. Restrictive licensing spread from the East African to the West African colonies, while state export monopolies spread from

West to East Africa.

Ideology alone might not have brought about such comprehensive economic controls had they not also suited influential interests in commerce and in the public sector. Private interests lay behind the introduction of restrictive licensing for cotton ginneries in East Africa and the official allocation of quotas tor the buying of exports in West Africa. Both of these measures led to much wider controls. The appeal of state controls to contemporary politicians is familiar, but in the context of Africa their appeal to the Civil Service was particularly important. The controls and the implementing organizations extended the role and power of ambitious civil servants, creating influential and lucrative positions and helping many of them to secure honours ranging from modest OBES to august GCMGs and peerages.

According to the perverse priorities of contemporary government, the creation of specific organizations and the expenditure of large sums of money can lead to recognition even if the money is clearly wasted, or activities run counter to their declared objectives or to acknowledged principles of policy. Conversely, achievement – even great achievement – goes unrecognized if it cannot readily be attributed to some specific action or to particular individuals. Thus no one received a high honour for the development of Onitsha, an important market town in Eastern Nigeria which grew steadily over several decades from insignificant beginnings (by 1950, its two principal markets had some twelve thousand separate sales outlets). The rise of Onitsha was made possible by the establishment of public security, which was virtually non-existent in Eastern Nigeria as late as 1890 but was taken for granted by the 1930s. Numerous honours, however, flowed from the establishment and operation of the Marketing Boards, whose activities impoverished the farmers and promoted political tension and corruption.

The economic controls were generally unrelated to their declared objectives, notably the promotion of the economic and social advance of the population at large. Indeed, they damaged the interests of the population for the benefit of certain sectional interests. Their introduction was especially anomalous in West Africa, where rapid and extensive economic progress had already occurred, very largely under the impetus of the private trading which many of the controls set out to inhibit. Progress there had, in fact, been so rapid that the changes it engendered set up problems of their own, as was observed by scholars of widely differing persuasions.[7]

5

State monopoly of export was introduced to West Africa very soon after the outbreak of the Second World War. A plan for the wartime organization of the cocoa industry was submitted to the Colonial Office, and in November 1939 it was accepted, with only minor modifications. Henceforth, the British government announced, it would buy all cocoa offered for sale in British West Africa. Its purchasing agency would have a statutory monopoly of export, and cocoa would be bought for the agency under a system of officially enforced quotas allocated to established merchants who would act as its buying agents.

The declared objective was to prevent the local price of cocoa from collapsing as a result of the shrinking market and the wartime shortage of shipping. But in that case there was no need for monopoly of export: a government guarantee to buy at a fixed price would have sufficed. And what need was there for quotas when the market was made unlimited by the government's guarantee to buy all cocoa for sale? The anomaly was evident in the very nature of the quotas, which were not for specified amounts but for specified percentages of the unspecified total quantity of cocoa bought by merchants on behalf of the government.

The quota system was an official version of the periodic market-sharing agreements of the leading West African merchants, which were designed to restrain competition and protect their trading margins. Merchants bought the principal export products in accordance with percentage shares agreed among themselves. Those who exceeded their quotas had to pay compensation to those who had bought less, the penalties being calculated roughly on the difference between export prices and variable costs.

These buying cartels, a recurrent feature of West African history, were generally unstable. Participants evaded their obligations, and the arrangements were unpopular with the farmers, who opposed them as best they could. The best known of the cartels, the Cocoa Buying Agreement of 1937 (known as the cocoa pool), had sparked

96

off the Gold Coast producers' strike (known as the cocoa hold-up), when for some eight months farmers refused to sell cocoa to members of the pool. For a period trade was practically at a standstill. After protracted negotiations between the authorities and representatives of the merchants and the farmers, the merchants agreed to suspend the pool, but not to abolish it, a situation which continued until the outbreak of war.

The plan accepted by the government had been put forward by the Cocoa Committee of the Association of West African Merchants (AWAM), a cartel headed by the United Africa Company (UAC), a powerful subsidiary of Unilever. The buying quotas it imposed were to be based on past performance, mainly on market shares in 1935–7, and were identical with those of the 1937 cocoa pool, even in minor detail. The main difference was that the new statutory body, with its penalties and rewards, could force merchants to comply with its terms, making the system watertight. Most important of all, it would exclude newcomers.

Previous cartel agreements had frequently been undermined by established traders who were not party to them, and also by the emergence of new competitors, known as interlopers. On the eve of the Second World War, the most dangerous interloper in living memory had recently emerged as a formidable competitor to AWAM members. This was A. G. Leventis, former General Manager of one of the largest companies within the UAC group. In 1937 he was dismissed from his post but, supported by Barclays Bank and by a firm of Lancashire textile exporters, he set up his own company in the Gold Coast within a few weeks of his dismissal. Although trading conditions in 1937–9 were unpropitious because of the cocoa hold-up and the 1938–9 depression, A. G. Leventis and Company had progressed rapidly.

After some transitional arrangements, the cocoa export monopoly was handled under the Colonial Office by the West African Cocoa Control Board, which subsequently became the West African Produce Control Board (WAPCB). At first Leventis was given no quota, but after protest to the Colonial Office the firm received a modest allocation.

After the Japanese conquest of South-East Asia, export monopoly was extended to cover oil palm produce (palm oil and palm kernels) and groundnuts, and eventually also cotton. Here again, monopoly

97

of exports was coupled with a system of statutory buying quotas. The ostensible ground for the extension of export monopoly was the urgent need to expand supplies of vegetable oils and oil seeds to replace those lost in the Far East. Thus, while the rationalization for the cocoa export monopoly had been a threatened collapse of the price because of excess supplies and a shrinking market, the rationalization here was a threatened deficiency of supplies – an exactly opposite problem for which the same solution was offered. It should have been obvious that monopoly of export and buying quotas were not required to increase supplies. Indeed, such arrangements were bound to reduce supplies, as producers received lower prices from a monopoly than from buyers in competition with one another.

In West Africa this effect was compounded by the fact that the Produce Control Board received far lower prices from the Ministry of Food than were paid for comparable supplies from elsewhere. In addition, the Board systematically withheld from the producers an appreciable share of the proceeds by specifying low prices to be paid to producers by the buying agents (the merchants). The quota system stifled competition among these merchants so that the farmers rarely received more than the prescribed minimum price.

Thus it was the desire of merchants for statutory quotas that brought about the export monopolies of West Africa. Far-reaching economic controls had been established (ostensibly at any rate) as temporary wartime measures. But the familiar forces of self-perpetuation soon asserted themselves, and the controls were extended in scope and duration. Soon after the war, the authorities in the United Kingdom and West Africa announced that the export monopoly of the West African Marketing Boards would be maintained. In 1946, the British government announced in a White Paper that the official export monopoly over West African cocoa would continue indefinitely; and in 1948 the government of Nigeria announced the continuation of state export monopolies over all Nigerian crops. The declared purpose of these arrangements was the stabilization of producer prices, to be achieved by fixing prices in advance each season, shielding producers from short-term and cyclical price fluctuations.

Both during and after the war, the authorities stated that the export monopolies would on no account be used for taxing producers by withholding money from them. In fact, the system developed into one of exceedingly heavy taxation. During the war, the Boards had already begun to accumulate sizeable surpluses, and this process escalated greatly between the end of the war and the end of colonial rule. The ability of the authorities to tax the farmers derived from monopoly of export, which enabled them to pay the farmers far less than the market price for their products. Most were small-scale farmers, many with annual incomes of only a few pounds; they were, in effect, made to pay taxes at rates equivalent to those levied in Britain only on the very rich.

The system was handed over *in toto* to the incoming independent governments. The West African Marketing Boards served as a model for similar organizations throughout British Africa and in various other British dependencies. In all of these areas, the state export monopolies served as prime instruments for politicizing life, for increasing the power of the rulers over their subjects and for providing them with a major financial power base. (The Gold Coast–Ghana Cocoa Marketing Board served this role for many years for Nkrumah.) The vast funds of the Boards, hundreds of millions of pounds, accrued to people who had previously thought in terms of modest sums at most, and who had little experience of government and little or no sympathy for the majority of the governed. The operation of the Marketing Boards in the closing years of colonial rule clearly violated the formal undertakings given by the British government and the local administrations.[8] When on separate occasions this point was put to Oliver Lyttelton, then Colonial Secretary, and to Sir Andrew Cohen, then head of the African Department of the Colonial Office, each of them justified this policy in almost identical terms by saying that there was no future anyway for the peasant in Africa.[9]

6

Import licensing was another form of economic control in which chance events affected developments far beyond their immediate impact. During the war, the import trade in West Africa was highly profitable under a régime of import restrictions and in the absence of effective consumer rationing and retail price control. In such circumstances, a régime of restrictive import controls conferred windfall profits on some intermediaries. The grant of a licence to import goods was virtually a gift of money to the recipients and to the traders who were fortunate enough to be able to buy supplies from them at the controlled price. The importers and the favoured traders between them obtained the difference between the landed cost of the goods and their price in the uncontrolled final transactions with the consumers.

The prospects of large risk-free profits resulted in persistent excess demand, and a scramble for import licences and supplies at controlled prices. If traders sold below market-clearing prices they had to ration supplies to their customers, a situation which elicited charges of favouritism and led to tension, particularly when favoured customers could so readily re-sell their allocation at higher prices.

Import licensing was introduced in the Gold Coast soon after the outbreak of war and remained in force during the early post-war years. Its scope and severity varied from time to time, but it tended to become increasingly comprehensive. It was applied relatively leniently to imports from sterling area sources, or to imports for which shipping was more readily available (some ships would otherwise have carried only ballast on the inward journey, since most West African exports were much bulkier than imports). Because neither the Colonial Office nor the local government had the required experience for administering the controls, the authorities relied for this purpose on AWAM, which was both a cartel of merchants and a trade association.

AWAM therefore effectively determined import control strategy. This was important in such matters as the extension of licensing to supplies which made no substantial demands on shipping or foreign exchange, and in the choice of criteria for allocation of licences (whether, for instance, 'past performance' should be based on a merchant's total imports, or on the imports of a particular commodity, or on imports from a particular country in the selected base period). From 1942, decisions in these matters consistently favoured AWAM members and specifically discriminated against A. G. Leventis, although the principal AWAM advisor to the authorities was a man of unquestioned personal integrity and had no personal animosity towards him.

From its start in 1937, A. G. Leventis and Company progressed rapidly in the import trade and by 1939 was a major importer. It

100

continued this progress until licensing became extensive around 1941, and to some extent even thereafter. The firm succeeded in tapping new sources of supply in the Far East, South Africa and South America. From 1942, these supplies were increasingly subjected to official restrictions even when they required no foreign exchange, or came in ships carrying ballast. In spite of these restrictions, often plainly discriminatory, the firm continued to prosper and expand.

Between 1945 and 1948, the tensions engendered by import licensing and the attendant excess demand escalated rapidly as a result of two unrelated events whose effects were compounded by their fortuitous coincidence.

In the autumn of 1945, UAC and some other AWAM firms made formal representation to the government alleging wholesale corruption in the operation of import licensing in favour of A. G. Leventis and Company and some other Levantine and Asian firms. The government appointed the Martindale Commission to investigate the matter. Its chairman was a judge of the High Court of the Gold Coast. After a few weeks of perfunctory work, the Commission reported that Leventis, and to a lesser extent the other accused firms, had bribed key officials on a scale which subverted the operation of import controls. Leventis and members of his staff, who were shown the report a few days before publication, promptly protested that its major findings were untrue. One of the accused officials threatened to sue the Commissioners for libel; his passport showed that he was not even in the Gold Coast at the time when he was alleged to have improperly issued an import licence to Leventis.

The government nevertheless published the report. Its publication was followed by the intensification of an already virulent press campaign against the government and AWAM, of which the principal instrument was the *Accra Evening News*. This major local newspaper was edited by Kwame Nkrumah, who had recently returned to the Gold Coast and who attained national prominence through this campaign.

In those days, West African press campaigns were apt to be virulent. This one differed from others in that its charges were highly specific and well documented, and the government was forced to appoint a second Commission with Mr Eric Sachs (subsequently Lord

101

Justice Sachs) as sole Commissioner. The Sachs Commission, in effect a retrial of the case, began its public sittings in the autumn of 1947. The press campaign continued during its hearings, which for weeks on end regularly brought out information damaging to the government, to AWAM, and to the Martindale Report.

The Sachs Report, published in 1948, effectively overturned the major allegations of the Martindale Report. It supported some residual charges of corruption, but these were of such minor importance that the government decided to drop the case. These events raised the political temperature in an already highly charged atmosphere.

The press campaign was financed at least partly by Leventis, who also supplied it with documentary material, some of it derived from AWAM merchants who disapproved of UAC's behaviour. Leventis was well aware that in supporting the press campaign, and Nkrumah's newspaper in particular, he could be unleashing forces which might prove uncontrollable and eventually greatly damage expatriate trading interests, including his own business. He thoroughly understood the threat to his position posed by the unrelenting hostility of the top management of the United Africa Company, an organization then at the peak of its power in West Africa. But he was convinced that without such a campaign he could not get the Martindale findings reversed.

Other events exacerbated political tension in the Gold Coast during this period. In the summer of 1947, as a result of one of the recurrent sterling crises of the early post-war period, the Gold Coast government announced that during the 1947–8 cocoa season there would be substantial import cuts. This unexpected reduction was certain to cause hardship and unrest. Moreover, since the reductions were effected through specific controls, they were bound to increase windfall gains to the trading firms who received licences, and to their privileged customers, thus exacerbating the tensions inherent in specific controls unaccompanied by effective consumer rationing.

In the winter of 1947–8 an acute supply shortage developed, leaving a persistently wide gap between open market prices and the prices at which imports were available to merchants and their preferred customers. There was incessant agitation for more licences and supplies, accompanied by accusations of profiteering and

102

favouritism. These developments coincided with the hearings of the Sachs Commission and the press campaign which accompanied it. In January 1948 the tensions produced civil unrest, which rapidly developed into full-scale riots and looting.[10] Some twenty people were killed in police actions designed to control the riots.

These events accelerated constitutional changes in the Gold Coast, enhanced Nkrumah's political position, and gave him the edge over the older generation of political leaders. In 1946 he had been practically unknown in the Gold Coast; by late 1948 he was a leading, even a dominant, political figure. The events served to undermine the position and self-confidence of the government, but they had a further less obvious but not insignificant result. Some politically uncommitted civil servants, including the then Governors of the Gold Coast and Nigeria, inferred from what had taken place that the power of the European merchants was excessive, and that it was their activities which were responsible for political tension, including the Accra riots. They threw their weight behind the maintenance of wartime controls, especially the continuation of the Marketing Boards. This response was misplaced; without the official controls, AWAM had little effective market power, especially in the import trade, as was clear from the rise of Leventis. The political tensions had in fact been largely brought about by the wartime controls and their method of operation.[11]

7

Economic controls of the kind we have described produce certain familiar results. They restrict both the range and variety of external contacts and the movement of people and goods within the territories. They retard the spread of new ideas, methods and attitudes; and they reduce incentives and opportunities. They divorce output from consumer requirements and obstruct the effective deployment of resources. They hinder the expansion of efficient producers and the establishment of new enterprises.

They also have less familiar and more lasting consequences. Close economic controls politicize economic life. The enhanced significance of political power intensifies the struggle for it, which is bound in turn to affect the deployment of people's energies and resources, a major determinant of economic performance in any society.

The great increase in the prizes of political power has been a major factor in the frequency and intensity of political conflict in contemporary Africa and in the rest of the less developed world. Extensive politicization sets up centrifugal forces, a result predictable and evident in multiracial and multitribal societies. These then have to be suppressed, by armed force, by the rulers who wish to exercise power over the largest possible areas. The Nigerian civil war of 1967–9 presents an example of these sequences.[12]

African tribal and cultural diversity was not created by the colonial powers. It was largely a legacy of the long period of isolation of small backward societies, the poverty of communications, and the lack of public security in pre-colonial Africa. The limited government of the period before the 1930s restrained the centrifugal forces: the policies initiated in the late colonial period helped to unleash them.

The departing colonial governments and their successors had agreed that the colonial boundaries should be the frontiers of the independent countries. This suited the African politicians, who did not wish to surrender any part of the country which they were about to take over. The political and financial benefits which accrued to rulers and administrators from the operation of economic controls reinforced this predilection. And since the rulers of the individual states are reluctant to relinquish any part of their power, the controls have also inhibited economic co-operation. Hence the hollowness of high-sounding African organizations which serve little purpose beyond seeking to impress the West, and providing jobs, publicity and perquisites for African politicians and civil servants.[13]

8

Despotism and kleptocracy do not inhere in the nature of African cultures or in the African character; but they are now rife in what was once British colonial Africa, notably in West Africa.[14] This is rarely stated publicly, although it is evident and familiar to those who know the scene. Many traditional African societies had leaders who acted capriciously, but they often governed rather lightly and with the voluntary consent of their subjects. And commercial relations informed by mutual confidence and trust in personal integrity have long been commonplace between Africans themselves, and between European merchants and their African customers and suppliers. It was the British policy of the closing years of colonialism that contributed greatly to the creation of a new political climate in which despotism was likely to emerge and corruption bound to flourish.

CHAPTER 7

Industrialization and Development: the Nigerian Experience

1

In his substantial monograph, *Industrialization in an Open Economy: Nigeria 1945–1966*,[1] Professor Kilby reviews the establishment and growth of manufacturing industry in Nigeria since about 1945, and examines at length the official policies designed to promote industrialization. He is knowledgeable, and brings to his task an unusual combination of qualifications. His temperament and outlook are scholarly, and his intellectual integrity is apparent throughout. He attempts to do justice to opinions different from his own, and when he notices evidence or opinions inconvenient to his position, he does not attempt to minimize them, let alone to conceal them. He is at home in those parts of macro- and micro-economic theory usually deemed relevant to development economics. He knows Nigeria well, and he understands the value of direct observation and the use of primary sources. These qualifications have resulted in the production of a book of considerable general interest and importance.

It is a work which presents a convenient opportunity to assess major aspects of economic policy in what was the largest British colony and is the most populous African state, and also to draw the attention of economic historians to certain characteristics of the development literature which limit its value and which often escape the notice of non-specialist readers.

Kilby's primary concern is with the establishment of various manufacturing industries in Nigeria to supply the home market, mostly in replacement of imports and chiefly behind high tariff walls; and with the establishment of manufacturing facilities in Nigeria for the processing of agricultural produce, mainly for export. These are the principal topics of Parts 2–5 of the book, its core. He is a sure guide in this field. He uses economic analysis carefully and is well informed about the specific developments he describes and assesses,

106

including the government policies behind them. He attempts to place his treatment in a wide context by providing a description of the general background of economic activity in Nigeria (Part 1), and by rounding it off with a discussion entitled 'Strategy for Industrialization' (Part 6).

We focus first (sections 2–5 below) on Kilby's distinctive insights and contributions. These lie in the description and analysis of specific aspects of the process of industrialization. We shall refer subsequently to certain aspects and implications of his treatment of the wider context.

2

Professor Kilby computes and emphasizes the high level of the protective tariffs which shelter several major industries. He correctly notes that it is effective rates of protection that matter rather than nominal rates. The effective rate expresses protection as a proportion of the value added domestically, while the more usually quoted nominal rate relates the tariff to the value of the product: in measuring the extent of the effective assistance to domestic manufacturing activity, the value of imported raw materials and imported intermediate goods (which are usually admitted duty-free, or attract duty at much lower rates than the final product) needs to be deducted from the value of the output. Kilby shows in an interesting table (p. 48) that in several textile-manufacturing activities the rate of effective protection in 1961 exceeded one hundred per cent; this means that the domestic value added (at world prices) was less than the value of the domestic resources used (similarly calculated). He shows that conventional tariff-making, which focuses on nominal rather than effective rates, ensures that 'the shallower manufacturing processes receive a proportionately larger protective subsidy than do industries contributing a greater net output' (p. 47). The conventional pattern of tariffs favours assembly operations and the provision of finishing touches to consumer goods, and can obstruct the subsequent establishment of intermediate and capital goods industries.

Much of the discussion in the theoretical literature on the welfare effects of tariffs, including the various arguments for tariff pro-

107

tection, assumes that the tariff-makers both are well informed about the relevant costs, markets, and production possibilities, and determine tariff structures in a disinterested manner, designed somehow to maximize some nebulous social welfare function. These assumptions are unrelated to reality. Thus Kilby shows that in Nigeria, as elsewhere, the protective subsidies to encourage new industries were over-generous, partly at least because government was unable to check the claims of interested parties. Moreover, as is usual elsewhere too, there was generally 'intense political pressure to push through the project from the region of its prospective location' (p. 49). Kilby notes that 'it is a reflection of the intensity of regional political pressure for industrialization that an impartial tariff commission or similar technical body, first proposed in the mid-1950s, has not been established or even seriously discussed' (p. 49, n. 2).

Kilby shows that before the late 1950s few industries were developed to meet domestic demand in Nigeria, although the market was often large enough to support a number of medium-sized factories. But from about 1958 there was a marked increase in private investment in local industry, notably by suppliers of imports (both overseas manufacturers and local merchants). This was at a time when the general economic and political climate was deteriorating, with increased political uncertainty and a decline in public administration stemming from 'internal political problems connected with tribalism and regional separatism, and the rapid expansion of government services coupled with an even more rapid Nigerianization' (p. 54).

Kilby explains this increased investment largely as a response to the increased competitive pressure which faced overseas suppliers (that is, both foreign manufacturers and the merchants who distributed their products), chiefly as a result of the greater attention given to the expanding Nigerian market by an increasing number of foreign suppliers. He considers the 'positive entrepreneurial response' to threats to one's market 'is to protect one's stake in the market by going into local manufacture. The competition from other sellers is eliminated by virtue of the protective tariff' (p. 55). Thus he suggests that the prominence of established suppliers of imports in local manufacturing reflects not only such familiar advantages as knowledge of the market, established contacts and possession of capital, but also and particularly the operation of a market strategy stemming from the desire of local merchants and overseas suppliers to protect their share of the market. Kilby does not argue that the first entrant into a manufacturing industry in Nigeria necessarily scooped the whole market; others might follow suit. But presumably because of economies of scale and possibly because of restrictions imposed by government (for example, on the number of expatriates allowed to work in the country), the number of suppliers established behind the high tariff would be materially smaller than the number of suppliers who would otherwise be willing and able to export to Nigeria. 'For the price of an industrial investment . . . a seller can transform the competitive market he currently faces into a monopolistic (or oligopolistic) market. . . . Hence for both the overseas manufacturer and the distributing merchant firm, the optimum solution to mounting competition and threatened markets will often be the establishment of a local factory' (p. 55).

Kilby develops and discusses his hypothesis with considerable skill and extensive reference to particular industries and firms. He does well to present and emphasize this point, which is often overlooked, and whose significance extends beyond Nigeria. At times he does not argue his case in sufficient detail, and he may have stretched his hypothesis too far. He does not specify precisely enough why other suppliers do not take advantage of the protective tariff, nor does he examine possible motives (other than the market strategy he emphasizes) for the desire of former suppliers to establish local operations. Some suppliers of imports may have considered that the advent of complete political independence in 1960 would make manufacturing locally an economic or political necessity for their continued operation, or would in various ways present exceptional opportunities for locally established producers, even in the uncertain situation which was developing. But on the whole, Kilby's account of the motives behind the establishment of local manufacturing activities by former suppliers of imports is convincing; at the very least it draws attention to the importance of market strategy.

He notes two important corollaries of his hypothesis. First, to the extent that income tax concessions were designed to induce new investment in industry, they may have been largely gratuitous, since the motivating force for many new investments was different from that envisaged in such legislation. Second, competition in the new industries tends to be non-existent or weak; indeed, this situation often provides the inducement for local investment by a pioneering firm. Hence some of the most adverse effects of over-generous tariff protection are not even partially offset by the subsequent development of internal competition. Kilby observes further that policies designed 'to promote maximum employment and training of Nigerians' have included highly restrictive immigration quotas for expatriate employees. These restrictions have 'prevented new exporters to Nigeria from establishing sales offices prior to a possible industrial investment' (p. 133), and have weakened the incentive to new entry otherwise provided by high protective tariffs. Here, as frequently elsewhere in the book, Kilby's description and analysis show how one type of policy measure impedes or renders impossible the achievement of its ostensible objectives or those of other policy measures. However, he does not always point the moral clearly.

Kilby himself does not suggest that all investments in import-substituting manufacturing activities were induced by threats to the market of established importers. He refers to several other industrial investments where 'the motive was the classical attraction to a profitable market opportunity rather than the compulsion of competition' (p. 72). In several instances the investing firms already had business interests in Nigeria. In other instances the entrepreneurs had no previous activities in that country. The latter category includes 'reputable, long-established manufacturing companies seeking an outlet for redundant equipment'. The 'outstanding case' in this sub-category was an American textile firm, Indian Head Mills, which 'promoted a £2.4 million textile venture at Aba to which it contributed £72,000 in cash and forty-year-old machinery officially valued at £688,000 in return for 70 per cent of the equity' (pp. 76–7). This venture, unlike many others, has been highly successful.

There is an interesting account of the activities of machinery merchants as investors and of the resulting projects, known as 'turnkey projects' (pp. 77–9). Kilby describes the 'rash of "machinery-sale public-investment" projects', in which the merchants had a small equity interest associated with a big sale of new (if not up-to-date) machinery. He explains that the public investment

110

projects were mainly political in their motivation, and that their results were seriously damaging: 'The drawbacks of this type of public investment are the extensive promotion of political and personal corruption, inflated capital costs (by 100% or more), serious external debt-servicing problems, and money-losing investments' (p. 78). And as was to be expected, the selection of the projects and of their location was made on political grounds, with little or no regard to economic efficiency; and the machinery merchants, unlike those manufacturers of machinery who have interested themselves in industrial projects, were unable or unwilling to supply or ensure on a continuing basis the necessary co-operant managerial and technical skills (or were not requested to do so). According to Kilby, this lack was the 'key factor in explaining why not a single turnkey project in Nigeria was earning a profit as of December 1966' (p. 79).

The discussion of the turnkey projects covers a large part of the industrial activities of state enterprises. Kilby reports that 'the regional Development Corporations, the agencies responsible for government-run industrial enterprises, reveal similar tendencies for public undertakings initiated during the 1950s, whether managed by Nigerians or hired expatriates: excessive over-staffing, sluggish response to competition, unresolved technical problems, profitless operation' (p. 79). He points out that this was in marked contrast to the joint ventures with foreign firms which undertook the management of the ventures and took a large part of the risk. Kilby's treatment is so austere, however, that he fails to note the unconscious irony of the designation 'Development Corporations' – most of whose investments 'are earning negative returns' (p. 168).

3

Apart from manufacturing industries which produce goods (largely substitutes for imports) for the domestic market, there are industries which process domestic products for export. These industries are discussed in Chapter 5 of his book, which deals primarily with the production for export of palm oil. Our discussion will be similarly confined.[2]

Professor Kilby provides a brief history of the palm oil industry in Nigeria, and gives a good account of the various methods used in the

111

extraction of the oil from the fruit. He describes (p. 154) the changes in the composition of different grades of palm oil exported in the 1950s, which, in accordance with common Nigerian usage, he terms 'a spectacular improvement in quality'. He then shows clearly that, contrary to what is sometimes claimed, the introduction of the Pioneer oil mills (one of the four methods of palm oil extraction now available in Nigeria) had little to do with this improvement.[3] He rightly attributes the change to the operation of the price incentives introduced by the Marketing Board in paying producers grade differentials much wider than those obtaining in export markets (where the Board resold the oil bought locally). He notes rightly that this practice was made possible by the fact that the prices paid by the Board to the producers were far below world market prices: as the Board had the sole right to export, it was able to divorce both the level and also the structure of producer prices from those ruling in the export market. Kilby notes correctly that one effect of the under-payment of producers – a policy which is still being pursued – was that it reduced total output as well as export earnings: 'Total proceeds to Nigeria from palm oil exports would undoubtedly have grown faster under a régime of higher producer prices and smaller [grade] differentials' (p. 156).

This observation is correct. The sustained under-payment would have had the adverse effects indicated by Kilby, besides other adverse effects not noted by him, even if the money withheld from producers had been used more productively than in the financing of projects, political parties, and persons favoured by the most influential politicians and administrators. (Kilby himself notes the negative returns of the bulk of the projects financed by the various organizations supported by the Marketing Boards.) And although he notes that palm oil exports and thus export earnings were affected adversely by the under-payment of producers, he does not emphasize that this example, as well as others in the book,[4] makes clear that the volume and value of exports (and also of imports), and hence the balance of payments, depend heavily on government policy, and are not the inevitable consequences of forces outside the control of government. The contrary view is implied or asserted in much of the development literature, in which the alleged lack of control of the governments of less developed countries over the volume and value

112

of their primary exports is adduced as the basis for the necessity of a variety of restrictive government policies. Indeed, much of the current development literature urges that substantial development of less developed countries is bound to involve balance-of-payments difficulties, a view which carries the inference that a country which is not experiencing such difficulties is growing less fast than it might otherwise do. Yet many less developed countries, as well as those now regarded as developed, have had long periods of effective growth without balance-of-payments difficulties; and, of course, many countries have had balance-of-payments difficulties without experiencing economic growth. Kilby himself accepts at times the insubstantial notion that development involves balance-of-payments difficulties, as for instance when he writes that the petroleum industry in Nigeria can free Nigeria from the 'binding constraint' of 'deficient foreign exchange earnings', an allegedly 'growth-attenuating' constraint which is 'typically the lot of developing economies' (pp. 15–16).

Kilby does, however, illustrate neatly a very interesting and little-known implication of the Marketing Board's policy. He carefully examines the economics of the four different methods of palm oil extraction and explains why 'the native method continues to be the predominant technology employed in palm oil extraction throughout Nigeria' (p. 154). The explanation is as follows. The technically more advanced methods extract a higher proportion of oil from the fruit than the more labour-intensive native method. The prices for palm oil which prevail in Nigeria are determined by the producer prices set by the Marketing Board, and these are far below commercial values in the world market. At the lower levels of price prevailing in Nigeria it does not pay processors to use the technically more advanced method which extracts more oil, although it would pay to do so if the prices obtainable for oil were the commercial values, that is, the export price minus cost of transport and distribution. Kilby notes that there is a loss to the economy 'both with regard to export earnings and domestic consumption – of thousands of tons of palm oil left in the discarded fruit pulp each year' (p. 165), and he estimates that at the level of output in 1965, the volume of what he calls 'recoverable' oil lost to the economy was about 61,000 tons against total exports of 156,000 tons.

4

His chapter on indigenous enterprise in manufacturing (Chapter 10) ranks among the most comprehensive surveys yet published on indigenous manufacturing industry in Africa. It is, however, strongly weighted towards the activities of government agencies. One would have preferred to read more about individual indigenous entre- preneurs, whether stories of success or of failure. Most of the chapter is a review of the activities of various official agencies which assist indigenous enterprises, primarily by heavily subsidized loans or grants. The review of these activities is largely one of failure. Money was available for the promotion of subsidized enterprises. But various elements indispensable for their successful operation were not, such as adequate management of the labour force, separation of personal and business expenditures in the conduct of private enterprises, adequate provision for future contingencies and systematic investigation of market conditions. In many instances assistance was granted for purely political reasons.

Professor Kilby puts forward quite definite views on the general reasons for these failures, though he chooses to express them in a rather convoluted form and modish jargon: 'The development of certain requisite entrepreneurial characteristics, relating to perfor- mance in the organizational and technological spheres, is being impeded by traditional socio-cultural factors common to all of Nigeria's ethnic groups' (p. 341); and again: 'the weight of the evidence points to lack of absorptive capacity on the part of the aid-recipients [recipients of official subsidies] as the principal bottle- neck' (p. 336). He also notes, more directly, that what he has been analysing is 'an important instance of the homely truism that economic development involves far more than mere economic change' (p. 342).

This emphasis on socio-cultural and personal factors is welcome. But it is probable that in Nigeria (as in other former British dependencies in Africa) the process of development, and especially the emergence and spread of attitudes, conduct, and institutions required for the progress of the exchange economy, would have been both eased and accelerated if the incomes of agricultural producers

114

had not been so drastically reduced over decades by the policies of the various statutory Marketing Boards. The surpluses of these Boards – in effect export taxes – provided much or most of the resources of the so-called Development Boards and Corporations. And the general politicization of economic life, to which the policy has contributed greatly, has reinforced the operation of socio-cultural factors impeding development.

There is much of interest in Kilby's emphasis on socio-cultural factors, and in his often illuminating account of the operation of certain institutions designed to enlarge the scope and improve the performance of manufacturing activity, such as the formal education system and applied industrial research. His account of the operation of these institutions is again a recital of well-nigh uniform failure of the officially sponsored transfer of methods and institutions which have functioned well, or at least tolerably, in the West, but which in the wholly different conditions of Nigeria have proved ineffective at best, and more often harmful. Thus there is a brief but perceptive discussion of the high costs and damaging effects (some of which will extend into the future) of the extremely rapid expansion of formal primary education.

A chapter entitled 'Industrial Relations and Wage Determination: Failure of the Anglo-Saxon Model' discusses at length the failure of the Nigerian trade union movement, governed by an ordinance drafted by a British expert on trade union affairs:

> The absence of an environment and a set of felt-needs similar to those which produced the Anglo-Saxon model has far-reaching implications for its institutional transfer. The sustained loyalty and discipline required of union members, which was built up in an earlier era only after long years of struggling for recognition, cannot be generated when the antecedent goals pursued by the trade union lose their primacy. . . . The development sequence – the learning process – required to make collective bargaining viable as a technique for determining wages is denied to present day underdeveloped countries. (p. 302).

Kilby recognizes that 'under existing circumstances in underdeveloped countries' labour organization serves as little more than 'a political instrumentality for channelling the protest of privileged wage earners' (p. 303), who are 'already a highly privileged minority' (p. 301) employed in the public sector, and by the large foreign-owned firms. He notes the economic consequences of the 'politicized

115

Anglo-Saxon model'. Wages in some sectors have been substantially increased, thereby reducing the volume of employment there compared to what it would otherwise have been.[5] Income differences between town and country have been widened, and this has 'aggravated the rural exodus and urban unemployment (with all of its political ramifications)'. And, compared to the 'pre-existing non-unionized situations the politicized Anglo-Saxon model has resulted in worsened, rather than improved, industrial relations' (p. 303).

The results and implications of the expansion of the formal education system and of the attempted establishment of Western-type trade unions are specific instances of a wider range of problems, namely the extreme difficulty, or at times impossibility, of transferring institutions between societies profoundly different in historical background and experience, values, institutions and customs.[6] It is easy to transfer the name and form of an institution, but not the spirit and experience which animate it. Failure to recognize this important fact is regrettably common in much of the development literature, and often derives in part from an insufficient appreciation of the time perspective in discussions of both the background and the prospects of economic development in less developed countries. Such a foreshortening lies behind the belief, or at least the frequent statements, that most less developed countries can reach the level of material attainment of the West in a few years or decades. It lies also behind the oft-encountered statement that the production of export crops has not contributed to economic development because the producing countries are still far behind North America, Britain or Western Europe in their economic attainment.

Inappropriate use of statistics is another instance of the pitfalls involved in attempts to apply Western methods and concepts to the conditions of less developed countries.[7] In this field also, Kilby recognizes some of the difficulties but fails to draw the requisite conclusion. Thus he notes that population statistics of Nigeria are subject to wide margins of error; and he explains why he prefers his estimate of 37.1 million for the population of Nigeria in 1963 to the official census figures of 55.6 million (p. 4). Yet he at times presents detailed statistics which are misleading, such as percentage changes in total gross domestic product and in gross investment, expressed to the nearest fraction of one-tenth of one per cent, or statistics of the numbers of the school population or of employment in certain activities expressed to the nearest digit. In fact, the statistics of national income and of capital formation in Nigeria, as in other less developed countries, are subject not only to vast inaccuracies of compilation, but also to large biases and errors reflecting certain problems of concept and measurement which affect the orders of magnitude of the figures, and often result in errors of several hundred per cent.[8]

Recognition of the extent of these errors and biases should help to put into perspective discussions often found in the academic and official development literature which present arguments and proposals pivoting on changes of one to two per cent in *per capita* income or *per capita* investment in less developed countries or in the less developed world as a whole.

5

In the last chapter of the book, 'Conclusion: A Strategy of Industrialization', Professor Kilby draws on two decades of experience of industrialization, and considers the 'costs and returns of alternative ways of deploying resources between industrial and non-industrial production and between different uses within the industrial sector' (p. 345). We shall show that there is much of interest and value in this discussion but that it is nevertheless seriously marred by a failure to see the problems and prospects of industrialization in historical perspective.

Kilby begins from the position that the 'great majority of underdeveloped countries will have to place major emphasis upon import replacement' if they wish to increase the extent of their industrialization. Much of the chapter is about ways and means of achieving such industrialization most efficiently in terms of costs and benefits. He disposes effectively of two major strategies for import substitution encountered in the literature on development economics. These are based on the theories of balanced growth and unbalanced growth and are associated with the names, respectively, of Ragnar Nurkse and Albert Hirschman.

His examination of the two theories leads him to reject the two strategies and to suggest a 'wiser policy', which in effect boils down to the prescription that measures should be taken 'to increase productivity and to reduce cost'. He rightly says that 'cost reduction widens the markets for those industries that achieve it; their expanded output, conjoined with increasing agricultural production (particularly exports), progressively generates the growth in income which enlarges all markets' (p. 351). He goes on to consider the question, granting the priority of measures to reduce cost to raise efficiency, 'what criteria should be used when selecting imports for domestic replacement?' (p. 352). The general answer is that the criterion should be a 'slightly qualified comparative cost principle'. One should choose those products 'whose potential domestic unit cost is lowest relative to the duty-free import price' (p. 352), allowing, however, for such factors as 'the estimated increase in factor productivity which results from the transfer of technology and organization [from the protected industry] to other industries' (p. 353).[9]

This may not strike the reader as amounting to much of a strategy for industrialization, especially because Kilby does not examine the problems of forecasting future costs of imports and of domestic production. However, it is a merit of his treatment that he resists the blandishments of taking over elegant and elaborate theoretical constructs and arguments for protection as if they were obviously applicable to the circumstances of and conditions in the country in question, and readily capable of being translated into practical policies and decisions. Moreover, in developing his proposed strategy, Kilby makes several important points.

He considers at some length the case for deliberately introducing more capital-intensive methods in manufacturing industry, although less capital-intensive methods are economically more efficient – a case argued on the grounds that, on certain assumptions, the choice of the former promises 'a larger capital stock and higher consumption at some future time' (p. 354). He comes out strongly against this case and concludes that 'cost-minimization should take primacy over all other criteria' (p. 361). He questions effectively the conventional assumptions behind the choice-of-technique analysis. In particular, he scrutinizes the crucial 'assumption that of the income generated by a particular investment, a substantially larger share of profits is likely to be reinvested than of wages', and concludes that although the assumption is 'correct in its narrow formulation, the situation appears

118

quite differently in its institutional setting, at least in Nigeria' (p. 360). He points out that in Nigeria the capital-intensive industries are likely to be foreign-owned companies or state enterprises; and he examines various disadvantages of relying on these categories as sources of productive saving. He also observes that small-scale labour-intensive industries in Nigeria have attracted many indigenous private firms, thus eliciting savings for investment in these activities. He also correctly notes a point familiar to economic historians but neglected or even denied in much of contemporary development economics, namely that productive saving and investment do not necessarily depend on the level of income (that is, they are not simply dependent variables of income).

Kilby explains also that capital-intensive enterprises have tended to remain 'technological enclaves' (p. 358) with little or no effect on the quality of indigenous entrepreneurship, management or industrial skills. He contrasts their limited influence with that of the 'small, modestly financed, individual or family-owned concerns (predomi-nantly Levantine)' in which men are substituted for equipment. The example set by such firms has given rise to 'hundreds of Nigerian firms' in such activities as the manufacture of soap and umbrellas as well as saw-milling, rubber-crêping and metal-working (p. 358). He argues, in consequence, that 'the encouragement of smaller-scale, labour-saving foreign investment (probably Levantine) will maximize the techno-logical and managerial carry-over from the foreign sector' (p. 362). It is refreshing to find the advocacy of such a realistic but unpopular policy: it is unrealistic only in the sense that it is unlikely to be implemented. It is equally refreshing to find the final sentence of the book rejecting nostrums still widely canvassed as indispensable for the progress of less developed countries in the face of much contrary evidence: 'There is good reason to believe that a shift in emphasis in the development effort from maximizing public investment and the savings ratio to improving organizational efficiency will yield a higher rate of economic growth in the short run, and create necessary conditions for the absorption of new technology over the long run' (p. 364).

6

Professor Kilby is to be commended for his refusal to repeat widely held views about economic growth and the means for achieving it.

Nevertheless, in some important respects his treatment is less careful than might have been expected from his generally cautious and critical approach.

Kilby agrees with 'virtually all students of the subject' that 'a certain amount of industrialization is likely to be a necessary condition for successful economic development' (p. 345).[10] But the statement is invalid however many students of the subject might agree with it. To begin with, Kilby does not specify what phase or period of development he has in mind. And again, while manufacturing is often a concomitant of certain phases of economic development, it is neither a generally necessary nor a sufficient condition for it. Moreover, as Kilby's own survey of industrialization in Nigeria amply shows, the growth of subsidized manufacturing industries is more likely to retard economic development than to promote it. There is nothing in the nature of manufacturing activities to suggest that the enlargement of the manufacturing sector will by itself result in economic improvement, when the required resources have to be diverted to it by a subsidy from other activities.

Kilby adduces, albeit rather briefly, three reasons for the unwarranted presumption in favour of subsidized industrialization. These stem from supposed drawbacks in reliance upon primary production: 'a low income elasticity of demand for primary products, possible disruptive instability in export earnings and, most important, limited transmission of technological and organizational stimuli from primary production to other sections of the economy' (p. 345). His advocacy of industrialization rests primarily on the third of these arguments. We begin with a brief consideration of the first two points.

A low income elasticity of demand would not warrant transfer of resources to less productive activities unless it were not only low but also negative.[11] If the income elasticity of demand is low but not negative, it means no more than that these activities will not be as advantageous as they would be if the income elasticity were higher. And even if the elasticity were negative, this would not imply that an early transfer of resources out of primary products would be economic without considering comparative costs and market conditions of different activities, the cost of the transfer of resources and the advantages or the benefits to be secured by continuing for a while

120

with primary production.

The principal exports of primary products from Nigeria, as from many other less developed countries, are industrial raw materials (such as petroleum) and relatively high-grade foodstuffs (such as cocoa), for which the income elasticity of demand is unlikely to be low, and is certainly not negative. But even if the income elasticity of demand for these exports were negative, such a situation would not warrant subsidized industrialization. It might warrant expenditure on increasing the flexibility of the economy to facilitate shifts of resources out of primary production, if and when the market were to contract.

Fluctuations in export proceeds may serve as ground for accumulating reserves in periods of prosperity and drawing on them in periods of depression. But they do not represent a valid ground for subsidized industrialization (which implies the taxing of other activities) so long as the income from the taxed activities exceeds that which could be secured over a comparable period from manufacturing. And this is the condition implicitly assumed in the argument that manufacturing, to be viable, needs to be subsidized at the expense of the rest of the community. Moreover, here again expenditure on increasing the flexibility of the economy would seem a more appropriate policy than the promotion of subsidized manufacturing.[12]

7

Elsewhere in the book (pp. 44-6 and 352) Kilby refers explicitly to two other arguments for state-sponsored manufacturing. First, that factor prices do not reflect opportunity costs (especially that wages in organized activities often much exceed social opportunity costs); and second, that manufacturing industries yield pervasive external economies (external economies are cost reductions in some activities brought about by expansion of other activities). He considers these arguments inapplicable to Nigeria. They can, however, be rejected on wider grounds also.

The first argument implies that wages in manufacturing exceed the economic cost of labour to the community, measured by the productivity in alternative employment. But such a situation would call for a revision of the methods of wage determination rather than for state assistance to manufacturing, especially since wages are often institutionally determined in various other activities as well (for instance, large-scale commerce as well as public employment and construction work), and also because manufacturing is already subsidized by the pattern of government expenditure in less developed countries which almost always favours the urban communities and tends to benefit manufacturing. And, even if there were surplus labour in agriculture in some clearly defined and pertinent sense (which is by no means generally true in less developed countries), whether as a result of institutionally determined wages or for some other reason, it would not follow that subsidization of manufacturing, especially for import substitution, would provide more employment than, say, encouragement of agriculture or improvement of communications. The presumption is the other way.

The second argument is also defective. There are few authenticated instances of genuine external economies yielded by manufacturing. In any event, subsidized industrialization implies the contraction of the taxed activities, with a loss of potential external economies stemming from those activities. It would need to be established that the external economies yielded by the subsidized activities exceed those lost in other directions. For instance, even if subsidized import substitution would yield appreciable external economies, these may well be outweighed by external economies lost by the curtailment of export activities, including the processing of agricultural product for export; and the latter categories are likely to be more suitable for the conditions of many less developed countries. No attempts appear to have been made so far for any country to compute the balance of such economies from subsidized manufacturing; and it is doubtful whether such an attempt would be worthwhile. Moreover, calculation of the economies secured would also have to take into account the costs resulting from the political and administrative repercussions of subsidized industrialization.

At one point Kilby writes that there is only 'one viable justification for protection – to subsidize an infant industry during an initial period in which it is achieving cost reductions as a result of learning' (p. 45). However, even the *prima facie* validity of this argument hinges on external economies, as otherwise businessmen could be expected to

122

cover the cost of the learning process themselves. Moreover, there is no reason why such cost reductions should be more pronounced in manufacturing than in commerce or in the production of cash crops.

8

Professor Kilby's advocacy of assisted industrialization in Nigeria is based primarily on the contention that there is a limited transmission of technological and organizational stimuli from agriculture to the rest of the economy, contrary to what he expects from manufacturing industries. In his discussion, however, he has taken an unduly restricted view of the interaction between agriculture and the rest of the economy and, partly for this reason, fails to note major implications of subsidizing manufacturing at the expense of agriculture, especially for export. The methods and implications of the financing of subsidized industrialization in Nigeria at the expense of agricultural producers need to be examined at greater length; and we may note that much of the argument applies to similar policies pursued in most less developed countries, though rarely in such an extreme form as in Nigeria.

Kilby notes in several places that subsidization of manufacturing in Nigeria has been made possible by the substantial and sustained under-payment of farmers, that is, by paying them much less than the market value of their crops; and, in addition, the prices of manufactured goods bought by them have been raised as a result of government policies. While Kilby notes at times that these policies have retarded the expansion of capacity and of agricultural production, he nevertheless neglects major economic results of these policies.

Kilby's treatment ignores the implications of the incomplete penetration of the Nigerian economy by the money economy, and by the attitudes and institutions appropriate to it. There is a large extensive margin of cultivation in Nigeria outside which agricultural activity is still largely restricted to subsistence or near-subsistence production. Large-scale taxation of agriculture to finance industrial development has served to retard the expansion of agricultural production for the market. It has thus retarded the monetization of the economy, the economic integration of the country, and the familiarization of people with the attitudes and practices appropriate to an exchange economy, which are in turn necessary for the development of the motivations, patterns of conduct, and outlook required for successful conduct of small- and medium-scale commercial and industrial activities. And the production of cash crops, and the trading activities associated with this process, are more appropriate for the development of the required attributes than the promotion of subsidized manufacturing by taxes borne by other sectors of the community, especially farmers. Production of cash crops and trading activities are more closely related to people's traditional pursuits than is industrial activity, so that the difficulties of developing attitudes and habits appropriate to an exchange economy are not compounded or exacerbated by the difficulties of simultaneous acquisition of unfamiliar industrial techniques. And manufacturing emerging from these activities is generally far less costly in terms both of conventionally measured economic costs, and of social strain, than is industrialization attempted directly from subsistence or near-subsistence agriculture.

In Nigeria, even more than in many other less developed countries, the spread of attitudes, aptitudes and institutions appropriate to an exchange economy is at least as important for economic progress (including the growth of viable manufacturing) as is the advance of technology and organization emphasized by Kilby.

The effects of the under-payment of agricultural producers have been compounded by the restriction of the supply of cheap imported manufactures through high protective tariffs and restrictive licensing, especially of imports. Many of the products affected are highly important inducement goods. The role of such products in the expansion of agricultural output will be familiar to economic historians.

The heavy taxation of farmers has also restricted the market for manufactures, and it has obstructed the progress of industries processing agricultural products both for the domestic market and for export; that is, the development of types of manufacturing particularly appropriate to an economy such as Nigeria. Kilby has noted how official policies have curtailed such development, and in the case of palm oil processing have retarded the adoption of capital-intensive methods which were readily accessible to indigenous entrepreneurs,

124

and which in this instance were economically efficient. He could have added that the exceedingly heavy taxation of export crops has greatly restricted the scope of saving and investment, both in agriculture and outside it. It has also inhibited the extension of trading activity which in Nigeria, as in many other ldcs, has often served as a training ground and as basis for subsequent development of viable industrial enterprises.

9

Some of the oversights noted in the preceding section reflect in part the drastic foreshortening of the time perspective in this book which we have already noted in the context of the transfer of institutions. Few of Professor Kilby's readers could be expected to realize how backward was Nigeria as recently as the closing years of the nineteenth century, when tribal warfare, slavery, and slave raiding and trading were widespread, and when there occurred well-documented instances of cannibalism. There were practically no schools and no man-made roads in the country. A large part of the population had never seen a wheel. Understanding of this background is necessary for an appreciation of the transformation which has already taken place, and for an assessment of the policies designed to promote further advance. The pertinence of this background has not been sufficiently noted in the writings about Nigeria since the Second World War, or in the policies pursued there.

Disregard of major components of the background unfortunately also affects other aspects of Kilby's treatment of recent history, including his references to Nigeria as an open economy (in the title of the book and elsewhere). He employs this term to indicate among other matters that the policies adopted in Nigeria ensured 'that Nigeria's internal price structure has been fairly closely related to world prices', and that 'the absence of extensive state intervention contributed to an open, market-orientated economy' (p. 1).

This characterization is astonishing in view of Kilby's frequent references to the policies of the Marketing Boards in keeping producer prices of the major export crops well below world prices. In fact, over the period reviewed by Kilby, the producers generally received only between one-third and two-thirds of the commercial value of their crops. At this time practically all agricultural exports were handled by state export monopolies. The establishment of industrial, commercial and transport enterprises was subject to official licensing; imports were closely controlled; manufacturing industry was widely protected, often at effective rates exceeding one hundred per cent; and favoured activities and enterprises received lavish cash subsidies.

So far from there being little state intervention in the economy, state control was so extensive that it amounted to large-scale politicization. This politicization of economic life has greatly exacerbated political tension and hostility in Nigeria, an ethnically highly diverse country which is indeed a collection of different societies and peoples with substantially different backgrounds and cultures. Kilby often refers to instances of corruption, large-scale misuse of funds, political and personal favouritism, and crass inefficiency in the operation and financial transactions of official organizations. But he does not convey adequately the extent and closeness of state control of economic life, and its far-reaching implications and results.

10

The merits of the book reflect Professor Kilby's scholarly disposition, technical competence and extensive reliance on first-hand material. Its occasional limitations, such as those we have noted, may reflect an inability to resist completely the influence of some characteristic flaws in the contemporary development literature which divert attention from simple fundamentals.

There are certain significant shortcomings widely encountered in the most influential development literature. An incomplete list of these would include the following: a neglect of the historical background and severe foreshortening of the time perspective; the disregard of alternative uses of resources and thus of cost (a characteristic example is the treatment of the resources of organizations such as development corporations or banks as additional resources rather than as resources transferred from other uses); the selection of variables on the basis of tractability to formal reasoning, or on the basis of political predilection, rather than for their

126

importance as agents or determinants of situations and processes; the neglect of the interaction of the conventional variables of economics with the parameters, and of the repercussions on the parameters of policies designed to operate on these variables (repercussions which are often, and perhaps even usually, far more important in their effects on development than are direct effects through the variables); the disregard of simple empirical evidence, reflected in such statements as that balance-of-payments difficulties are necessary concomitants of development; a neglect of aptitudes, attitudes, mores and institutions as determinants of economic attainment and progress, combined with the implied assumption that societies, groups and persons do not differ significantly in these characteristics; a failure to appreciate the implications of the incomplete monetization of the economy, their importance to economic development of the institutions appropriate to an exchange economy, and the corresponding neglect of repercussions of government policies upon these influences; and the neglect of the far-reaching effects of the politicization of economic and social life, an understanding of which is indispensable for an understanding of the bitter political struggles in many less developed countries, and thus of their history in the last few decades.

Some of these shortcomings have in places crept into Kilby's book, albeit primarily where he has attempted to place his specific concerns in a wider context. Their presence should not, however, obscure the considerable merits of his book. A measure of the author's achievement is that, despite some shortcomings, in most of these respects his treatment is greatly superior to that in what may be called the mainstream of the contemporary development literature, official as well as academic. He has produced a valuable account of some major policies affecting the establishment and growth of manufacturing activities in a large less developed country; and the significance of many of his observations extends well beyond the country which he knows well and which he has chosen to examine.

CHAPTER 8

The Economics of Post-War Immigration Policy in British West Africa

This chapter is based on a paper published in 1954. It deals with immigration policy in Nigeria and the Gold Coast, the combined population of which was over ninety-five per cent of that of the British West African colonies. Policy in the other two colonies, Sierra Leone and Gambia, was basically the same.

We have preserved the substance of the discussion throughout and have largely retained the present tense.

The passage of time, including the conferment of independence on the two countries, has not made the treatment obsolete. In fact, the controls on immigration have been greatly intensified and extended. The analysis of the inconsistencies in the proclaimed objectives of West African immigration policy remains unchanged. The pertinence of the analysis has indeed increased. This is so because restrictions on immigration have become much more widespread and severe throughout the less developed world, accompanied at times, as in West Africa, by restrictions on internal migration.

1

Immigration policy in Nigeria and the Gold Coast has been similar in essentials for the last decade or two, and the texts of the immigration ordinances in Nigeria and the Gold Coast, as well as of the principal regulations issued under them, are the same in all provisions of substance.[1] Administrative practice in the two countries is alike in aim and emphasis.

What follows is a review of the immigration policy and practices in these two West African countries, and an analysis of the economic effects and implications of the restriction on the entry and activities of

128

non-African immigrants. The discussion is not primarily concerned with suggestions for the amendment or reformulation of immigration policy. Nevertheless, it is critical in that it reveals inconsistencies in the presuppositions which underlie the present policy, and in that it emphasizes the economic costs of the policy, which are often not sufficiently understood or recognized by politicians, administrators or the public in West Africa. It may be noted in passing that although it is confined to West Africa, the discussion is of wider relevance because the effects of immigration control in West Africa are much the same as those of similar policies which are being followed in some other so-called underdeveloped territories.

The discussion is limited to immigration policy insofar as it affects established expatriate trading firms, individual traders and their employees, as well as prospective entrants into trade. Traders and their employees are quantitatively by far the most important group affected by immigration policy.

2

Expatriates are admitted into West Africa only if the immigration authorities are satisfied that their entry will not harm the economic development of the local African population. The authorities have powers to limit the numbers admitted, and these powers are used extensively. The general aim is not to increase, and if possible to reduce, the number of non-Africans in these territories. The authorities are given a large measure of discretion in deciding whether the activities of a would-be immigrant are likely to benefit or to obstruct the progress and interests of the local population.

In general, prospective immigrants who intend to engage in industrial activities are more likely to be admitted than those who intend to become traders or merchants. But the immigration control is not equally severe in respect of all prospective traders. Thus the establishment by expatriates of new firms to engage in the direct importing of merchandise into West Africa is not completely barred, though the permission of the immigration authorities must be obtained even here. A prospective entrant into direct importing may be refused admission if, for example, the authorities consider that he has insufficient capital. On the other hand, the establishment of new

129

expatriate firms in the distribution of imported merchandise, after the stage of first importing, is more rigorously checked. This is generally referred to as a bar against the entry of more expatriates into 'retailing' or local trade.[2] Expatriates are also debarred from the internal trade in local foodstuffs.

Retailing in this context has a different meaning from that ordinarily attached to the term. It does not refer solely to the business of selling to the ultimate consumer. The official interpretation of the term includes transactions which are several stages removed from sales to the ultimate consumer. Considerable latitude is given to the authorities in determining whether a particular activity is wholesale or retail trading; the bar to entry into retailing is virtually complete. In general, any breaking of bulk of imported goods (meaning the division of a consignment into smaller lots) appears to be regarded as retailing, even though the size of the transaction makes it clear that it is several distributive stages removed from sale to the ultimate consumer.

The general administration of immigration policy is most restrictive in respect of Levantines and Indians, and especially of the former, who are probably the most numerous of the applicants for permission to immigrate.[3] They and their trading activities are generally the objects of a special degree of doubt and apprehension in the eyes of the immigration authorities.

The admission of expatriate employees of trading firms is also controlled. The size of the expatriate staff which may be employed by established trading firms is regulated on an informal quota basis, and the quota of each firm is broadly determined in accordance with the numbers employed in pre-war years. Applications for permission to engage new expatriate employees tend to be favoured if the numbers employed are within the quota.[4] Newly-established firms are given permission to employ expatriate staff in accordance with the requirements of their trade. The authorities have a wide measure of discretion in the detailed application of the guiding rules.

Immigration permits to employees are usually granted on condition that the recipient is engaged in a particular occupation or employed by a particular firm. And it is difficult for employees subsequently to change occupation or employment. An immigrant is practically prevented from starting a trading concern of his own. This is important because, in the past, firms established by former employees had sometimes developed into serious competitors of the established trading houses.[5]

3

The official immigration restrictions bearing on so-called retailing of imported merchandise (which, however, consists very largely of wholesale trading) have certain obvious and direct effects on these trades, as well as other less obvious but equally (if not more) important effects on the general trading situation. Immigration restrictions operate on so-called retail trading in three ways. The entry of new expatriate firms is practically prohibited; the expansion of existing firms is hampered by control over the immigration of non-African staff; and expatriate firms engaged solely in direct importing find it difficult, if not impossible, to extend their operations to include wholesaling and semi-wholesaling (i.e. resale to other intermediaries).

The direct result is to reduce the degree of competition and to strengthen the position of established trading firms whose activities extend beyond direct importing. These established firms include the large vertically-integrated merchant houses which play so important a part in the external trade of West Africa.

A principal assumption of the immigration policy has been that competition in the distribution of imports would be preserved by the entry of African intermediaries who would fill the gap caused by the exclusion of expatriates or the restriction of their activities. This assumes that African traders can adequately perform the necessary services relating to the distribution of imported merchandise. However, this assumption is invalid. There may well be sufficient Africans who can supply these services, but the excluded expatriate competitors could do so at lower cost and on better terms than those Africans who owe their trade directly to the shelter provided by the regulations. This follows from the fact that the regulations have to be used to exclude would-be entrants, and to curb the activities of existing firms. This conclusion is further confirmed by the difficulties of the large non-African trading firms in recruiting suitable local traders to take over some of their trading activities, or in diverting

131

business for political reasons from Levantine to African trading customers.

The entry of new expatriate firms into the activity of direct importing is not completely barred though it is controlled. But the restrictions on entry and on the expansion of firms in the stages of distribution subsequent to the importing of merchandise substantially affect the degree of competition and of concentration in direct importing itself. The total volume of trade in imported merchandise is likely to be reduced, because the efficiency of distribution is impaired by the regulation of immigration. The restrictions also make it more difficult for established expatriate firms not engaged in direct importing to expand sufficiently to become direct importers, and to compete with the large vertically-integrated merchant houses. Further, the market for the activities of new or growing non-integrated firms of importers is narrowed, a result which inhibits this possible source of competition in the import trade.

These results of the restrictions on expatriate enterprises are again not offset by the expansion of African businesses. The presence and possible growth of African firms in the non-importing stages of distribution are unlikely either to provide new entrants into the import trade or to provide so satisfactory a market for rising non-integrated importing firms. This conclusion is suggested by the higher costs and more modest qualifications of those African traders who owe their position to the operation of the restrictions. Their weakness in capital resources, combined with other disabilities, suggests that many of these traders are more likely to be tied to particular sources of supply, which tends to increase the difficulties facing new or small importing firms.

The local distribution of merchandise brought in by other merchants is probably the best apprenticeship for subsequent entry into the import trade itself. It may also provide a source of capital for the hard-working and efficient trader. Experience of the local market, knowledge of customers and the possession of capital are necessary in the West African import trade where credit has to be granted extensively and where lack of experience or capital tells heavily against the newcomer. The initial capital requirements for successful entry into external trade are usually heavy; but they are appreciably less for entrants who have local contacts, knowledge and experience.

Restriction of entry into local trading activities therefore closes or narrows a particularly suitable means of access to the import trade itself.[6]

The immigration restrictions reinforce the trading position of the established expatriate firms in the import trade, and buttress the high concentration which is a marked feature of the external trade of Nigeria and the Gold Coast. The restrictions on expatriate traders, and particularly on the entry of newcomers, strengthen an existing degree of concentration and reduce the efficiency of independent alternatives available to the customers. Even if these restrictions give African traders a larger share of the market in some of the later stages of distribution, this does not reduce the degree of monopoly or of concentration facing the customers. As a result of the immigration restrictions, all protected firms, both expatriate and African, operate in a less competitive environment, where profit margins tend to be higher and more secure, and where formal or informal price-fixing and market-sharing arrangements can be more effective. The rest of the African community – producers, con-sumers and other traders – obtain their services on less favourable terms. Moreover, the real dependence of the population on the large and established expatriate firms is increased because those Africans who owe their existence as traders to the immigration restrictions are not as effective or as efficient competitors as the excluded expatriates would have been.

It is often claimed for the immigration policy that any increase in the number of expatriate traders would strengthen the monopoly elements in external trade. As is clear from the foregoing discussion, this claim is without substance. Moreover, it is mis-leading to apply the term 'monopoly' to a situation in which the members of one race, nationality or tribe collectively are prominent in a particular branch of trade or industry, if they do not act restrictively or in concert.

Many West Africans protest against the commercial power of the existing expatriate firms, particularly against the power of the large United Africa group and other leading European firms. But they also protest against the admission or growth of other expatriate businesses which in the circumstances could offer effective competition to these large firms.

133

4

Any attempt to enumerate the specific economic functions performed by traders and trading operations is apt to distract attention from
the essential and pervasive influence of expatriate trading enterprise
in initiating and promoting the economic development of West
African territories. Sir Keith Hancock has justly discussed the
economic development of West Africa in terms of the extension of
the traders' frontier.[7] The part played by traders in the promotion of
economic progress is perhaps less immediately obvious today, but
hardly less valuable than in the past.

The productive role of trade is of great significance in so-called
underdeveloped economies. Trade conduces to the most economic
deployment of available resources and assists in the integration of
supply and of demand. It helps in the husbanding of scarce resources,
and in the development of exchange between geographically
scattered regions in territories where transport, communication and
storage facilities are poor.

Trade promotes the growth of resources in a variety of ways. It
widens markets, promotes specialization and increases output both
for export and for local consumption. It serves to bring new
commodities to the notice and within the reach of actual or potential
producers of cash crops, making it worth their while to produce for
sale, and at the same time providing a market for their produce. This
process encourages production and the extension of capacity, more
especially the extension of the acreage under cash crops. People have
access to a wider range of both imported and domestic goods, which
tends to reduce the cost of living and the extent of price fluctuations.
These sequences promote both the accumulation of capital and its
effective use. Increased output creates a surplus for accumulation
and improves the real return on capital.

Trade also brings into prominence and influence a type of trader
entrepreneur accustomed to the ways of an exchange economy –
notably the habitual and systematic use of money. These trader
entrepreneurs are more likely to accumulate savings and place them
in productive employment than are other sections of the population.

The immigration restrictions in West Africa inhibit the productive role of traders both in the deployment of resources and in promoting their growth. The effects are pronounced, because expatriate traders usually possess some special entrepreneurial, managerial or technical skills, and are generally more industrious and frugal than the local populations among whom they work.

The trading activities of European and Levantine enterprises are an important source of capital formation. This is so even where the owners or employees enter West Africa with nothing. They accumulate capital in the course of their activities by consuming less than their earnings, and this is as useful in raising production and providing employment as if it had been brought in by them in the first instance. In practice, the capital generated in the course of these activities is likely to be more productive and therefore more useful than capital brought in from outside. Capital generated locally will be deployed by people familiar with local social and economic conditions, and therefore it is more likely to be used effectively.

The working experience gained by traders frequently enables them to be aware of opportunities in spheres other than trade itself. As in most other underdeveloped countries, most of the relatively successful industrial enterprises have been founded by the trading firms. Examples include saw-milling, tanning, brewing, the manufacture of plywood, soap, furniture, groundnut oil and stationery. The capital and skill employed in these activities provide substantial employment for African labour.

The implications of the curtailment of the activities of Levantines are particularly notable. They are representative of a class of immigrant which has played an important part in the process of economic development in many underdeveloped countries. The Levantines in West Africa are rarely highly educated. But they are resourceful, industrious, enterprising and exceptionally gifted in the perception of economic opportunity. They are prepared to accept lower remuneration than Western European personnel, and the services they render are often performed at correspondingly lower cost. Levantine traders, or firms employing Levantines, can therefore operate on a slower rate of turnover and on a smaller volume of trade than would be necessary to sustain British or Western European personnel.[8] Thus they can operate in relatively backward and sparsely populated areas. Restrictions on the expansion of

Levantine activity inhibit development at the margin and retard growth of the market economy.

5

If trading activity were an immutable fixed volume, then the exclusion of expatriates would necessarily increase the amount of trade handled by Africans. But no such simple conclusion follows once it is recognized that the trading activity in a country is not a predetermined given quantity.

The control of immigration retards the growth of the volume of trade and economic activity in West Africa, and therefore it works directly against the economic interests of African consumers, producers and workers. Moreover, it is almost certain that the volume of trade handled by African traders is smaller than it would be if there were no restrictions on expatriate trading. In the absence of restrictions on expatriate traders, Africans who owe their existence or prosperity to the controls would be displaced, or would have lower incomes. But the expansion of trade would benefit African traders in those stages of trade or distributive activities which would remain in African hands even without these controls. Quantitatively, the most important of these activities are the concluding stages in the distribution of imported merchandise and the initial stages in the assembly of export produce. On all but the most extreme assumptions, the absolute volume of trade handled by Africans would increase, even though some of their number would be displaced in various branches of trade. This conclusion can be stated even more emphatically if account is taken of the effects of the activities of expatriates on the progress of the economy as a whole.

Those who benefit from the activities of the expatriate traders rarely appreciate the nature and origin of their advantages. But those who may or do suffer from expatriate competition are highly sensitive to this threat.[9] The displacement of some African traders as a result of the less restricted entry of expatriate firms would be obvious both to themselves and to the public generally, whereas the benefits would be widely diffused, and some (the benefits resulting from the growth of the economy) would permeate the economy only gradually. The displaced African traders are likely to be those who operate on a substantial scale, while the benefits (largely unperceived) would accrue mainly to small-scale traders and to final users of trading services. This localization of losses would give rise to the impression that the subservience of Africans to the expatriate traders had increased. It would also strengthen the impression that the African population was cut off from the outside world by an impenetrable layer of alien trade.

For these reasons it would be difficult for the administration to reverse its immigration policy or even to modify it materially. The vocal section of the public is recruited largely from among those African traders who benefit, or at least appear to benefit, from current restrictions.[10] The much larger numbers of Africans who would benefit from more liberal immigration policy are unlikely to appreciate the fact or the origin of the benefits. Moreover, they are largely inarticulate and without influence.

The West African administrations appear to be apprehensive of the political consequences of any policy which would increase the number of non-Africans. Yet it seems doubtful whether present policy reflects merely popular opinion and political pressures. In general, the authorities seem disinclined to inform their people of the full economic effects of the immigration restrictions. Administrators do not seem to recognize that the economic interests of different African groups are not the same, and that the special interests of sectional groups are not the same as those of the population at large. Moreover, the authorities seem to share the popular belief that an increase in the activities of expatriate traders (with the possible exception of those exclusively engaged in direct importing) diminishes the opportunities open to the African population. It appears that they are not clearly aware of the role of trade and of expatriate traders in promoting the growth of capital in suitable hands, and thus in providing additional employment for Africans. Immigrant traders are likely to be seen in a different light when it is realized that they provide opportunities for the local population rather than diminish them.

It may be argued that the economic disadvantages of restrictive policy are temporary, and that they need to be set against the advantage of the acquisition by sheltered African traders of experience and skill in the initiation and management of larger-scale

137

mercantile enterprises. Although some benefits of this kind may be expected, they are likely to be small in relation to the costs of the policy. Most mercantile skills may be acquired at much lower cost by Africans who obtain responsible employment in expatriate firms. Moreover, the experience and skill acquired in the shelter of restrictions are apt to mislead the beneficiaries, and to cause them to underestimate the difficulties and requirements of successful trading practice. Such an outcome is of some practical and political import-ance in emerging economies.

The previous discussion summarizes the principal conclusions that may be derived from economic analysis. On a somewhat different plane certain other considerations may be, and indeed have been, advanced in favour of present immigration policy. Thus it is argued that much African discontent derives from the knowledge and the rumour of the opulence of expatriate traders, and that the important part played by those communities in the economic life of the colonies is a grievance in itself. The feelings of dissatisfaction may not be assuaged even when it is realized, as it is very rarely, that the activities of expatriate traders are productive and that their wealth has not been secured at the expense of the population at large, whose incomes have in fact been increased.

Such considerations may well be relevant to policy. But it is also pertinent that hostility to expatriate traders is much more evident among politicians, journalists and larger-scale African traders than among the peasant producers and smaller traders. These latter largely inarticulate groups seem to be more concerned with im-proving their economic lot. They do not necessarily like expatriate traders, but they are interested in improving the terms on which they deal, and in extending the range of available alternatives. If they object to the expatriate traders their opposition often springs at least in part from a sense of dependence on the comparatively few expatriate firms; and this dependence tends to be increased by the restrictive results of the immigration policy.[11]

6

There is an incompatibility in the twin objectives of immigration policy, namely the maintenance of a homogeneous population in

Nigeria and the Gold Coast, and the promotion of the economic development of these territories. Some of the complications of a mixed racial society may be relieved by a restrictive immigration policy, but only at the cost of retardation of economic development and growth. And insofar as the major objective of immigration policy is the avoidance of a multiracial society, the appropriate course would be to restrict the total number of expatriate immigrants without special discrimination against those engaged in trade.

Concessions to demands for exclusion and restriction of expatriate activities tend, moreover, to have cumulative effects. In West African, immigration controls and the arguments adduced in their support encourage similar demands for restrictions on the internal movement of Africans and on their freedom to engage in trade and trade-related activities. The racial and tribal diversity of the populations of Nigeria and the Gold Coast furnishes ready pretexts for restrictive measures on inter-regional and even inter-district trade and migration, which has further unfavourable effects on economic progress.

It would not be appropriate here to attempt an assessment of the relative merits and demerits of a multiracial society, or to suggest which of the two objectives of immigration policy should take priority. But failure to appreciate the incompatibility of the two objectives only clouds the questions involved; and it contributes to policies of restriction even on internal movement, with a resulting fragmentation of these economies.

CHAPTER 9

Substance and Method in Development Economics: a Commentary on the Views of Professor Stern

1

It is unusual, and rarely appropriate, for an author to comment on a review article of his book in an academic journal, especially when the article appeared some three years after the book and the comment cannot appear simultaneously. I have nevertheless accepted the editor's unsolicited invitation to comment on Dr Stern's review article,[1] because much of his argument (which reflects major strands of the development literature) bears on wide issues of substance and method in development economics, and in economic studies generally.

2

Stern writes:

> Many of the arguments that are commonly advanced for the positions Bauer attacks are weak. The problem is that Bauer's attacks are often inconclusive because their target is some of these arguments and not the policies themselves. [pp. 191–2.]

There is no problem. To begin with, Stern is in error in implying that a policy can be faulted conclusively by economic reasoning and examination of evidence. This is erroneous, because assessment of a policy depends upon the probable results of different policies on the total social situation, and these are affected by many factors outside the specific purview of economics. And the choice between policies must also depend on value judgements. On the other hand, arguments claimed to be based on analysis and observation are appropriately examined on the same basis and are therefore capable

140

of conclusive rejection. It is for this reason that so much of my book examines arguments in support of policies: the critique can be conclusive. Moreover, some of the arguments, the weakness of which seems common ground between Stern and myself, have often been adduced by their academic authors in support of far-reaching domestic and international economic policies. Finally, contrary to Stern's suggestion, I discuss in the book a number of policies in some detail.

3

Stern takes me to task for not supporting by formal tests my rejection of the hypothesis of the vicious circle of poverty. He asks:

> How then might one test the hypothesis of the pervasiveness of vicious circles? Presumably it claims that various factors reinforce each other so that, on the whole, the standard of living of the poor, or poor countries, tends to grow more slowly than that of the rich. This implies that the dispersion of incomes or wealth in a country, and across countries, tends to increase or, crudely, the 'gap' tends to widen. [pp. 194–5.]

> It is a fair test of the *dominance* [Stern's italics] of vicious circles, however, to ask whether indices of cross-country dispersion of incomes have been increasing. [p. 195.]

The hypothesis of the vicious circle has nothing to do with the dispersion of incomes. Any suggestion that it does represents a radical shift of the argument. As the various quotations in my book amply demonstrate, the hypothesis states that poverty precludes material progress, that it sets up practically insurmountable obstacles to its own conquest, and that this cause supposedly accounts for a negligible – or even a zero – rate of growth through time. The notion is summarized in the phrase 'a country is poor because it is poor'. This is not my phrase, as Stern's readers might be led to believe (p. 195), but that of Nurkse and Myrdal, who instanced it as a succinct formulation of the concept. And they do so in publications quoted or referred to by me and listed by Stern. The notion of the vicious circle, though plainly invalid, is not 'imprecise' as Stern asserts (p. 195). On the contrary it is quite definite, as reference to the quotations will show; the ambiguities are Stern's own contribution to the discussion.

141

Moreover, the notion rests on a readily identifiable model set out in my book.[2]

Stern refers to other uses 'on a theoretical level' of the words 'vicious circle' (p. 195). The examples he presents share the feature of the standard formulation that they entail a zero rate of growth (or in one case a negative rate) in the economies subject to the vicious circle. A test of the theory, either in its standard formulation or in the form of the alternatives proposed by Stern, cannot therefore be based upon comparison with either economies: it must be based on the presence or absence of growth *within* the afflicted economies. Stern's test based on the inter-country dispersion of income is patently irrelevant. However, were it deemed relevant its implications would be nonsensical. For instance, suppose that in a two-country model both countries were growing rapidly but the poorer less so than the other. One would then have to infer that the poorer country was caught in the vicious circle of poverty, regardless of its level of income or its rate of growth. More generally, an increase in the cross-country dispersion of income is quite consistent with unprecedented rates of growth in all countries. On the other hand, if in the two-country model the income of the richer were to decline while that of the other remained unchanged at a subsistence level, one would then have to infer that the poorer country was not caught in a vicious circle.

I have explained at length that the notion of the vicious circle is inconsistent with the rise from poverty to riches of innumerable communities and groups throughout the world, and indeed with the phenomenon of development as such; that it is inconsistent with the past progress of developed countries (dcs) as well as with the more recent progress of many less developed countries (ldcs) across the less developed world; that there were groups in different parts of the world which had progressed little in recent decades, but that this could not be explained by poverty as such; that the common identification of a low level of income with a zero rate of change is erroneous; and that the notion of the vicious circle is refuted further by the presence in many ldcs of problems associated with rapid rates of economic advance (*Dissent on Development*, pp. 32–4 and 37–8). So much for the contention that my contribution to the discussion is minimal, and that all I offer 'by way of testing is one or two examples of countries that have grown relatively rapidly' (p. 195).[3]

To turn to the widening gap (as distinct from the vicious circle), Stern accepts the need for scepticism about the degree of aggregation implied in a division of the world into two categories (although after expressing this scepticism he nevertheless mentions estimates of the ratio of *per capita* GNP of the United States to that of Asia as a whole); he recognizes the pertinence of the distinction between absolute and relative differences of income; he expresses doubts over the accuracy of the available data; and he infers from available studies that the gap (in terms of dispersion) has not widened in recent decades. However, his discussion is rather diffuse and relies heavily on national income statistics of ldcs which cannot sustain the weight he places on them (a matter to which I shall return subsequently).[4]

The diffuse nature of Stern's discussion reflects partly the ambiguities of the concept of the gap which, unlike the vicious circle, cannot be pinned down precisely and discussed succinctly and neatly. However, the widening gap is a subject of sufficiently general interest in development economics, and sufficiently close to the concerns of Stern's article as well as to those of my book, to warrant some discussion here.

The gap as normally interpreted refers to differences in *per capita* incomes between the collectivity of ldcs and the collectivity of dcs. The concept of the gap, and the statistics usually quoted to indicate its magnitude and also the direction of its movement, are subject to major ambiguities and complexities which materially affect the significance of the concept. These problems are inadequately recognized in the literature, including Stern's article. I list here some of these limitations and ambiguities.

(i) Estimates and comparisons of *per capita* incomes involving ldcs are subject to enormous margins of bias and error, the magnitude of which is often overlooked and certainly is not conveyed by Stern's article. Even without taking into account wide errors in population estimates, the biases and errors in estimates and comparisons of incomes often amount to several hundred per cent. And these biases cannot be expected to remain constant over time for many reasons, including the relative decline of small-scale agriculture in the course of economic development.[5]

(ii) It is not usually specified whether the changing gap refers to changes in the absolute difference in *per capita* incomes, or to changes in their ratios. The two kinds of change often move in opposite directions and at different rates.

(iii) There is no clear discontinuity, no clear gap, in the international range of incomes, which means that the line of division between the two global categories is arbitrary. It follows from this that the extent of the difference is also arbitrary. Moreover, some countries, namely some of the oil states which are conventionally classed as less developed, have for years had *per capita* incomes which are among the highest in the world.[6]

(iv) The line of division between the two global categories is not only arbitrary but also shifting, because some ldcs have been promoted to the ranks of the dcs. Thus the composition of the aggregates which are being compared changes through time, and this precludes any simple assessment of long-term changes in differences in incomes between the two categories. The pertinence of this basic consideration is evident from the frequent historical changes in the relative economic position of different countries.[7] From this it follows that the idea of a widening gap is meaningless unless the time period envisaged is specified.

(v) Both the developed and the less developed world are huge, extremely diverse aggregates, the components of which are themselves heterogeneous collectivities. It is certainly misleading and largely meaningless to aggregate Chinese merchants of South-East Asia, Indonesian peasants, Indian villagers, tribal societies of Africa, Arabs of the Middle East, aborigines and desert people, inhabitants of huge cities in India, Africa and Latin America, and many other groups. Differences in rates of development within these aggregates are an aspect of this diversity. In recent decades many ldcs have grown much faster than many dcs.

Apart from these basic problems of concept and measurement, there are two further sets of considerations pertinent to worthwhile discussion of income differences and changes.

(a) Conventional statistics of *per capita* incomes do not take into account life expectation. The large reduction in mortality in recent years in ldcs has substantially increased life expectation there and has also appreciably reduced differences in life expectation between dcs and ldcs. A longer life expectation is an improvement,

144

as most people prefer to live longer and to see their children live longer.[8]

(b) Worthwhile discussion of income differences and changes, especially if it is to serve as a basis for policy, needs to consider the reasons behind these differences, and these reasons cannot be inferred from statistics. Statistics of income differences are no guide to understanding, let alone to policy.[9]

4

Stern writes (p. 198) that I do not demand total inactivity on the part of the government. This rather misplaces the emphasis. As I observed (pp. 90–2), performance of the extensive and difficult governmental tasks which I envisage (summarized by Stern on p. 198) would stretch or exceed the resources of all governments of ldcs, most of which neglect many or most of these functions while nevertheless attempting extensive economic controls. They try to plan but cannot govern. The governmental tasks specified by me, while exacting and complex, do not normally imply such close control over the fortunes and lives of individuals and communities as do some policies pursued in the name of central planning. The former are much less likely to provoke political tension or lead to inhuman policies.

Appropriate demarcation between state and private activity must be influenced considerably by specific local conditions. The scope deemed appropriate for government activity may be more or less extensive than the list I proposed. One can readily admit that it could include correction for so-called market failures. In fact my list, quoted by Stern, includes several large-scale governmental tasks on the grounds of the presence of significant externalities. Market failures arising from private monopoly could similarly be accommodated. But the implied corrections need not involve central planning or the establishment of state enterprises or statutory organizations.

Whether or not government activity designed apparently to correct for market failures in fact promotes economic efficiency and development depends on various factors. These include, among others, the capacity and motivation of politicians and administrators, the information available to them, and the political pressures on them. It cannot be taken for granted that in these matters politicians and civil servants in ldcs are omnipotent and omniscient, and dedicated to the improvement of living standards and the widening of opportunities for the population at large.[10] Moreover, many such corrective activities, especially in the form of state or statutory enterprises, contribute to the politicization of economic life and exacerbate political and social tension, especially in multiracial societies. These effects cumulate rapidly with an increase in the number of such corrective activities, whether genuinely or only ostensibly corrective. And the number and extent of state activities in the aggregate are greatly increased in most ldcs by state enterprises and other forms of intervention which cannot by any stretch of the imagination or analysis be attributed reasonably to the attempted correction, for instance, of market failure.

It is in this context that such activities as the Kenya Tea Development Authority (KTDA) should be considered (Stern, pp. 199–200). It may well be that taken by itself this specific state activity could be justified in terms of market failure, and that its implementation has been efficient. However, examples like the KTDA (insofar as the case for it rests on the need for redefinition of property rights, or the presence of externalities or high transaction costs) can be accommodated readily in my agenda for government activities, provided that the offsetting disadvantages of the kind just noted are not substantial. But even if the single activity passed the test, one would still have to take into account its contribution to the cumulative effects of the aggregate of state activity and state enterprises.[11]

Stern's discussion mentions neither the extent of any direct or indirect subsidization of the KTDA scheme, nor any feasible alternatives to the scheme. He also does not mention that smallholder crops, including rubber, coffee, cocoa, coconuts and tea, have often been produced and marketed in ldcs without official schemes. On the economic efficiency of the scheme all that we are told, rather irrelevantly, is that the 'tea produced on smallholdings obtained good prices in London' (p. 199).

The general considerations noted earlier in this section apply also to Stern's argument that central planning may be necessary to correct for the failure of individual savers to take sufficient account of the

146

relative valuation of consumption now and consumption of future generations (p. 201). Further, this particular issue has no bearing on planning as usually understood in the literature or generally practised in ldcs. Detailed planning is certainly not necessary for an increase in the savings ratio, which can be accomplished by quite different policies, as for instance the encouragement of voluntary saving or the running of budget surpluses. I may note parenthetically that that particular argument could be used equally to justify the conscription of labour.

Preoccupation with the analysis of market failure and the theory of corrective intervention is a notable feature of development economics. It is a sorry reflection that it goes hand in hand with large-scale neglect of the realities of government action and its results both for welfare and for development.[12] Many of the discussions in this field that imply or take for granted that government intervention achieves an ideal situation, or at any rate improves the actual situation, do not examine either the likely economic costs or the wider social and political repercussions of state intervention. All too often the writers contrast actual reality with an ideal situation, and simultaneously fail to distinguish between the probable, possible and conceivable outcome of their implicit or explicit policy proposals, or the actual outcome of their implementation.

This shortcoming of the development literature stands out in Stern's article. Thus, characteristically, he does not pause to note the dearth of the simplest consumer goods, including food, in many ldcs after years of central planning, and its persistence in the face of statistics recording impressive rates of growth. Nor does he consider such major issues pertinent to his arguments for central planning as the repercussions of the character and extent of state control on the social, political and personal determinants of development; the likely effects of the politicization of economic life in provoking political tension and influencing the direction of people's activities and resources; the inequality of power between rulers and subjects promoted by central planning; the ability of the government to restrict the choices of the population at large; the differences of interest between politicians, civil servants and their associates on one hand, and the rest of the population on the other; and the effects of controls in restricting both external contacts and domestic mobility,

147

and thereby the spread of new ideas, attitudes, methods, crops and wants.

The reader may be reminded that in the 1960s (that is, the period of the operation of the KTDA referred to by Stern), economic life throughout East Africa became increasingly politicized, a development not mentioned by Stern. There was extensive large-scale official discrimination against highly productive minorities, and extensive regulation of economic activity unrelated to the correction of market failures and the promotion of development (and also irrelevant to systematic reduction of income differences). In East Africa, as in many other ldcs, the economic position and prospects of large numbers of people, and sometimes even their physical survival, have come to depend directly on who is the government, and this situation inevitably influences greatly the direction of their activities and resources.

These matters relate to an issue of much practical and intellectual interest, namely the interaction between the factors customarily treated as variables in economic theory, and the factors treated as parameters. I noted this interaction in several contexts, including development planning, foreign aid and technical assistance. Their disregard by Stern is a notable omission.

5

Some of Stern's observations bear on wide issues of method in development economics and indeed in social studies generally.

In discussing the vicious circle, Stern refers to an error said to run through the whole of my book, namely the alleged claim that 'a generalization is destroyed by the production of a few counter-examples'. According to Stern, the appropriate method is to examine whether the statements criticized 'were valid in a statistical sense', or, where statistical testing is difficult, 'whether the balance of evidence pointed one way or the other'. He claims that I virtually ignore the first method and misuse the second – implying that I did not make 'a genuine attempt to balance the evidence' (p. 194).

No econometric exercise is necessary to refute the standard formulation of the vicious circle of poverty (see section 3 above). Further, in my treatment of this hypothesis I did not rely upon merely 'one or two examples of countries which have grown relatively rapidly' (Stern, p. 195). My examples were in fact drawn from the experience of a wide range of countries, both in the past and in the post-war period.[13]

Similarly, no elaborate discussion of cases and no econometric analyses are required to refute such notions in development economics as the contention that balance-of-payment difficulties are inevitable in the economic development of ldcs, or that their terms of trade deteriorate persistently, or that dcs have caused their poverty, or that central planning or foreign aid is indispensable for development. Examination of the alleged analytical basis of these ideas and a confrontation of these ideas with simple evidence are amply sufficient for their rejection. The difficulty in dealing with these notions is not that of analysis or of statistical testing, but rather of conducting a discussion without appearing to descend into triviality.[14]

In the context of a discussion of method, Stern's own treatment of the hypothesis of the vicious circle is of some interest. It will be recalled that he redefines the hypothesis by applying a test for it (changes in the extent of the international dispersion of incomes) which is unrelated to its standard formulation (that poverty by itself precludes material progress). The subject of discussion is shifted and changed.

The same method is evident in Stern's handling of 'Bauer's contention that aid may reduce thriftiness' (p. 207). Stern reports a finding in a statistical study of a 'negative correlation between capital inflows and domestic savings rate across countries'. For what this is worth, this finding supports the contention attributed to me, although I would not claim it as support. Stern, however, changes the basis of the discussion by writing that this finding does not imply that 'countries save less (out of total new resources – domestic production plus capital inflow) when they receive extra capital from outside'.[15] This of course is so; but it has nothing at all to do with the domestic savings rate to which the contention under examination refers. This contention is dismissed by Stern who, in fact, discusses something quite different. But he is not happy about the negative correlation between capital inflows and domestic savings rates and so he goes on to explain it away. I need not follow his attempt in detail.[16] It is sufficient to note that he goes some way towards undermining the type of statistical analysis contained in some of the studies that he uses to support his own views (on p. 208 for example), and which is central to the 'statistical approach' that he favours (p. 194).[17]

Stern might well have gone further. Little useful evidence can be obtained from cross-country statistics which relate not merely to different economies but to quite different societies. In cross-country regressions the results are mainly likely to reflect the vast differences in conditions, government policies or the myriad other factors that bear on material well-being. The volume of aid, or indeed a balance-of-payments deficit, may be associated with such factors, and so may spuriously appear significant according to the statistical tests which are inappropriately applied in such cases.

Much of Stern's criticism of my book involves statistics, and studies using statistics, of *per capita* incomes of ldcs. He acknowledges that the figures are inaccurate, but he writes that we must use them 'because at present they are all we have' (p. 197). This is not so. In many contexts in which national income statistics of ldcs are used, we have other pertinent statistics which are much more reliable (and informative), as for instance statistics of foreign trade and of life expectation. And we have, or should have, powers of observation and reflection to tell us that the national income statistics of ldcs often cannot mean what they purport to mean. I have already quoted from an article by Usher from which Stern has quoted only a part of a sentence which did not convey the thrust of Usher's findings. This was that the biases and errors of the conventional income statistics of ldcs amount to several hundred per cent, and that these statistics are largely meaningless, notably so for international comparisons. In a book published in 1969, Usher developed this theme at length, with a sophisticated argument based in part on detailed observation.[18]

Moreover, it has also been suggested by another reputable authority that these statistics are at times manipulated precisely in order to secure additional aid.[19] The econometric studies cited by Stern in support of his views are based upon changes in the *per capita* incomes of ldcs. It is a misuse of the methods of statistical analysis to apply them to such raw materials.[20]

Insistence on the usefulness of national income statistics of ldcs on the ground that they are all we have is a notable instance of the belief in indiscriminate quantification, whether sensible or merely pretentious. And such practices are damaging both because they conceal the radical shortcomings of the underlying data, and also because they divert attention from other ways of reasoning and of collecting and interpreting evidence, and indeed are apt to be used to discredit them spuriously.

CHAPTER 10

Further Reflections on the State of Economics

In an essay published in an earlier volume, I considered certain characteristics of the practices of economists and suggested how these may have become pronounced since the Second World War. I drew attention in particular to what I considered the disarray into which large parts of the subject of economics had fallen, and noted the phenomenon of the acceptance of major transgressions going hand in hand with increasing sophistication and genuine progress. In the present chapter, I elaborate a few of the ideas discussed in that earlier essay, and also introduce some further themes.

I shall illustrate my arguments primarily by referring to features prominent in the mainstream of post-war development economics. My professional preoccupations are not the sole explanation for this. Forces at work also in other branches of economics are perhaps especially observable in this branch of the subject, as will become apparent in the subsequent discussion.

1

In a passage in *The General Theory*, which has been quoted so often as to have become hackneyed, Keynes claimed that the ideas of economists, whether right or wrong, decisively influenced the conduct of politicians and the course of events. 'Indeed the world is ruled by little else.'

Welcome as it may be to the interests of economists and to their *amour propre*, Keynes' position is clearly untenable. For instance, most economists since Adam Smith, including Keynes, have advocated free trade, but this has not brought it about. Keynes' inadequate and parochial formulation neglects not only the influence of vested interests but also that of religious, spiritual and ideological forces.

152

The practice of governments of appointing economists as advisers may have helped to propagate the notion of the influence of economists, notably as governments appear often to follow their advice. In fact, particular advisers are often chosen because governments rightly believe that their advice would accord with what they wish to do in any case.

Emphasis on the role of economists in shaping public affairs and on the ideas of politicians, civil servants and businessmen also suggests that the influence is one-way. This emphasis neglects the impact of the outside world on the ideas of economists. And yet they are plainly affected by political, social and ideological forces, by established interests of various kinds, and also by developments in other disciplines. The interaction between economists and the outside world is reciprocal and not simply in one direction.[1]

Ideological, commercial and intellectual forces all affect the opinions and conduct of people, including economists. These forces may reinforce each other, or they may constrain each other's operation and influence. Keynes' idea of a straightforward one-way relationship is clearly unwarranted.

Over the last half century or so, outside influences have much affected the activities, themes, methods and findings of economists. Even an incomplete list of these must include the extensive politicization of social and economic life; the spread of egalitarian ideology and of the belief in environmental determinism; the much-increased importance of the media, and therefore of the influence of those working in it; the speed of social, scientific and technological change; and the prestige of the methods which have contributed to scientific and technological advance.

Economics has always been highly susceptible to external influences. Since the war, the subject has become even more responsive to the vagaries of change emanating both from outside the discipline and from within. There have been frequent abrupt and disconcerting changes of direction and fashion. This instability may have become more pronounced in recent decades, as a result of factors such as the proximity of economics to national and international political issues, which themselves change more frequently; a lack of poise induced by exaggerated claims for the subject; the confusion of the distinction between advancement of understanding and the promotion of policy; and perhaps also some major un-resolved methodological questions.

External forces also shape the subject and its impact in an indirect but highly significant manner. Ideas and findings which run counter to prevailing ideological and political sentiment, or to vested interests, are far less likely to be accepted or publicized than those that are more congenial to these forces. Thus the content of the subject and the acceptance, impact and survival of ideas are all greatly con-ditioned by influences emanating from outside the subject itself. Here is one example.

D. H. Robertson (1890–1963) contributed fundamentally to monetary economics. Some of his major ideas deserve resurrection and further development, particularly in view of the vast expansion of international banking, and the emergence of various forms of near-money or money substitutes. Yet few economists today know of his work, a small number indeed, whilst Keynes is a household name. This is presumably because Robertson's ideas did not and do not have the political and ideological appeal of the Keynes of *The General Theory*.

2

In the decades after the Second World War, the number of economists, the resources at their disposal and the volume of their publications grew rapidly throughout the West. For instance, by the early 1980s there were in Britain as many university teachers of economics as there had been undergraduates in 1939; and in other forms of tertiary education and in schools the increases were even greater. The large inflow of people and money was prompted by hopes, encouraged by economists, that the expansion would result in greatly increased understanding; and that this in turn would help to solve a wide range of problems including secular stagnation, un-employment and poverty in the West, and backwardness in the underdeveloped world.

This large-scale expansion took place during a period of pro-nounced increase worldwide in the politicization of life, including education, literature and the arts. The process was promoted and accompanied by a great increase in the influence of intellectuals including academics, the media, professional politicians, civil servants and professed or professional humanitarians. These groups were fast becoming significant components of the political nation in the West.

Politicization has reinforced the readiness to confuse advancement of knowledge with the advocacy of policy. By interest and inclination, many of the most articulate and effective members of the political nation are hostile to the market. Hence their readiness to advocate state control of the economy, and often even large-scale replacement of market activity by state activities. Further, many of them also are hostile to the West, in part because, in the contemporary world at any rate, prosperous Western societies are comparatively more market-oriented than are materially less successful societies.[2]

Some of these influences and their results are especially notable in those parts of the subject which have burgeoned since the war, such as Soviet economics and development economics. This latter subject

f the concept of underdeveloped rectly from a particular policy, umbilical cord binds develop- of foreign aid and also of other ators and advocates has been

Reality and Rhetoric by P. T. Bauer

ERRATUM

Page 155, lines 19—20:

For development *read* development economics

omotion of knowledge has been subordinated to the advocacy of policy, it would be impossible to account for the persistence and survival of evident errors of fact and logic in development economics. A partial list of these transgressions includes notions such as that poverty perpetuates itself (the vicious circle of poverty); that external contacts are economically damaging; that comprehensive planning is indispensable for development, that economic development must produce balance-of-payments problems; and that better-off societies, groups and individuals owe their prosperity to the exploitation of others. These opinions have often been advanced by prominent economists.

The subordination of knowledge to political purpose is not only evident but at times acknowledged. On three different occasions in three different countries, I heard academic economists defend the notion of the vicious circle of poverty on the grounds that, although invalid, it has nevertheless been invaluable in the advocacy of foreign aid.

The transgressions in development economics are not random: their thrust reflects systematic hostility to the operation and outcome of market forces, and accords with the views of influential groups within the modern political nation. The influence of these groups, including prominent academics, has been indispensable for the continued widespread acceptance of the simplest errors of fact and logic. These groups tolerate and shield crude lapses if that will help to discredit or to criticize the operation of market forces. And because these influential groups are not ready to expose patent errors, and indeed shield their propagation, any exposure or criticism, no matter how intellectually compelling, makes little or no impact either in the academic world or in political and public discourse. This lack of impact is facilitated by the flood of publications and communications of all kinds, by professional specialization, and by the multiplicity of people's concerns. Effectiveness nowadays too often depends not on what is written or said, but on what is repeated and transmitted.

The influential groups protect not only the invalid notions but also those responsible for them. Even when their statements have been conclusively refuted by evidence or exposed by criticism, the authors will continue to be acclaimed as experts so long as their stance accords with prevailing ideology or dominant vested interests. Thus, influential exponents of the vicious circle of poverty are still regarded as world experts on development or even as outstanding figures in the subject. The same is true of the proponents of the dollar problem as one of a persistent world shortage of that currency.

The case of the late Professor Paul A. Baran provides an informative example of the coexistence of professional reputation and the publication of crass mis-statements.

In Chapter 2 of this volume, I quote an extended passage from *The Political Economy of Growth* (1957). He wrote there unequivocally that there was no productive reinvestment of profits by enterprises operating in ldcs and, by clear implication, no productive investment either. Elsewhere in the same book he insisted that commercial contacts with the West perpetuated backwardness in the less developed world.[3] These statements form part of the central argument of the book and reflect his Marxist-Leninist position. Similar assertions remain frequent in the writings of Marxist-Leninist

156

development economists, and of exponents of the so-called dependency theory.

The reality is, of course, that both domestic and foreign enterprises operating in ldcs have reinvested profits on a large scale and for many decades in successful or promising economic activities. And it stares one in the face that the poorest regions of the less developed world are those that have few or no external contacts. Moreover, multinational enterprises which, in the demonology of monopoly capitalism, are the arch-fiends, are rarely found in these poorest regions.

For decades before the publication of Baran's book, the commodities produced by enterprises in ldcs were staples of world commerce in daily use throughout the United States – such as oil, sugar, coffee, tea, rubber and tin. Books and journals on the development of these industries, and on the part played in them by Western enterprise and capital, are in all university libraries in the West. (Stanford, where Baran taught, houses two specialized libraries on Third World affairs.) The activities of many of these enterprises are discussed regularly in the American press.

Baran, as already noted in Chapter 2, was full Professor of Economics at Stanford University from 1951 until his death in 1964, and was regarded as a leading authority on economic development. He wrote the chapter on economic development in the American Economic Association's *Survey of Contemporary Economics*, a publication designed to present the state of economics immediately after the war to members of the profession and students returned from the war. He received many invitations to lecture on development at leading universities both in the United States and abroad. His own book from which I have quoted is still used as a university textbook.

What would have happened if a market-oriented economist had made assertions so completely and obviously in conflict with reality as are those of Baran? He would have been ridiculed, and such professional reputation as he had would have been assailed.

Almost as much as development economics, the study of Soviet-type economies has emerged and flourished since the war. In much the same way as the literature of development economics, a large part of the literature on centrally-planned economies has contained propositions and assertions which conflict starkly with reality. The

157

achievements of central planning, especially in the Soviet Union and the People's Republic of China, but also in Poland, Romania and elsewhere, have been persistent themes of much of this literature, including publications emanating from Western universities and from official international organizations. Phenomenal growth rates and the large volume of productive investment in these countries have been freely reported and commended as examples. These achievements were attributed to central planning, which was held up as a model to be followed elsewhere.

Throughout the period of these eulogies, acute shortages of such necessities as food, clothing and housing were evident in centrally-planned economies. A large part of the allegedly highly productive investment was wasted, as was plain from the many projects that were not completed, and from the factories that worked far below capacity for want of raw materials, spare parts, demand, or distribution facilities. The commendations of central planning continued even after the rulers themselves had acknowledged the plight of their countries and the failure of past policies.[4] Events since about 1980 have, however, succeeded in reducing the flow of these commendations and the uncritical acceptance of the claims made for centrally-planned economies.

3

The proposition that price affects the quantity supplied and the quantity demanded is central to economics. Recognition of these functional relationships has been the hallmark of economists since the earliest days of the subject. Supply and demand analysis is widely and effectively used by economists in the elucidation of observed phenomena and in the assessment of the effects of changes in market conditions.

It is therefore all the more remarkable that so much of post-war economic literature has ignored the fact that supply and demand depend on price, and that a shortage or a surplus can never be discussed sensibly except in relation to price. The disfiguring practice of discussing supply and demand without reference to price may conveniently be termed price-less economics.

This practice is rife in development economics. In several publications I have noted it in such contexts as the operation of the state export marketing monopolies in West Africa and elsewhere, the formulation of development plans, and the advocacy of state-supported industrialization.[5] A current example of the practice is presented by forecasts of the level of rural unemployment in the less developed world on the basis of population trends and the amount of cultivable land.

The practice of price-less economics is not confined to development economics. Since the Second World War, much economic discussion of the level and incidence of unemployment and of balance-of-payments problems has been conducted without discussion of wages or of exchange rates. For instance, prospective unemployment in the United Kingdom more than five years ahead is being discussed in terms of demographic changes, without regard to wage rates and labour costs. (How would one explain the economic history of the last century and a half if demographic factors were a material determinant of the level of unemployment?) More generally still, the long-term prospects of entire economies in the West as well as in the less developed world have often been discussed without reference to the relative prices of labour, capital and land.

There is a readily discernible political thrust in the practice of price-less economics. The practice implies that government direction or control is indispensable for the effective deployment of resources. The same thrust is evident when economists, while recognizing that supply and demand are functionally related to price, argue that the responses of supply and demand to price changes are very small or very slow. For if this were so, it would be plausible to argue for government direction of resources and regulation of consumption on the ground that the market would involve unacceptably onerous social and economic consequences. Of course, economists who favour the market may be apt to overstate the extent and speed of market adjustments. But whatever the relevant elasticities happen to be, the difficulty of determining these elasticities in no way warrants the practice of price-less economics.

In much of the development literature, the practice of price-less economics has flourished side by side with the advocacy of the use of shadow prices. Shadow prices are imputed or estimated prices which purportedly reflect the social cost of resources more accurately than is done by market prices (because of so-called market imperfections, or of rigidities resulting from government policy such as exchange or wage controls). It is odd that this preoccupation with shadow prices should have emerged simultaneously with the practice of price-less economics. The explanation may well be that the thrust of both the neglect of prices and the advocacy of shadow prices is in the direction of government intervention.[6]

4

Since the war, there have been highly informative and illuminating advances in economics. Simultaneously, prominent economists have perpetuated the grossest elementary transgressions of fact and logic, both in the core of the subject and in their own fields of specialization. Over wide areas intellectual standards have crumbled. The queen of the social sciences is in danger of being dethroned by her courtiers.

I am not alone in my assessment of the state of economics.[7] But colleagues whom I respect have disputed the contention that economics is in disarray, or have even regarded this idea as offensive. Such reactions are inappropriate, even irresponsible. To paraphrase what George Orwell said in a different context, in economics we have sunk to such depths that statement of the obvious has become the first duty of thoughtful people.[8] Statement of the obvious, which by now often amounts to rediscovery, has become a major task. But this may well be a more appropriate task than extensive preoccupation with refinements, at times indistinguishable from trivia, on the so-called frontiers of knowledge. Some of these developments give every appearance of being blind alleys. Indeed, they are apt to obstruct progress towards an improved understanding of reality. This pre-occupation has in turn diverted attention both from the study of reality and from the exposure of transgressions.[9]

Academics especially need to insist on the obvious in the face of its neglect or denial. To encourage the intelligent exercise of the critical faculty should be the major, perhaps even the primary, task of university teaching. But the prevailing conditions in much of economics often preclude effective performance of this function. Teachers face unenviable dilemmas. How can one fairly assess a student's performance if what he says or writes is plainly untenable,

160

even bizarre, and if at the same time he can cite in support a leading academic or two?

5

It is not only in twentieth-century economics that the coexistence of rapid advance and evident deterioration within the same area or activity is conspicuous. It now requires fewer days to fly around the world than it required months to get around it in the nineteenth century. But since the First World War, many millions of people have found it much more difficult to leave or enter many countries than before 1914. Thus, even such a straightforward question, whether travel has become easier or more difficult, cannot be answered unequivocally. Again, transmission of information has been revolutionized, but there has been no corresponding improvement in what has been transmitted.

The phenomenal progress of science and technology in the twentieth century presupposes disciplined and connected thinking. Yet a widespread inability to establish simple connections is also a readily discernible characteristic of the age. A Nobel laureate has written that the Iron Curtain reflects the difference in temper and outlook between Eastern and Western Europe, born of centuries of oppression in the former. A moment's reflection shows that if there were such differences, the barrier would not be necessary. Academics conduct elaborate studies about mass unemployment, and they do so in institutions which have for years been chronically short of secretaries, porters and cleaners at going wage rates. It is said by many that the Third World has not enough food for subsistence and survival, and the same people also complain about the rapid growth of population there. It is also often said that the Third World is destitute, and desperately short of material resources, and yet at the same time that it presents a threat to the West. Intelligent, articulate university students in Singapore write that external contacts inhibit development, when it is these contacts which have transformed Singapore from an insignificant fishing port into a major industrial and commercial centre. And they write also that without integrated rural development, planning agricultural advance is impossible, when the transformation of neighbouring Malaysia

161

without such policies provides readily observable evidence to the contrary.

The ability to undertake connected thinking in subjects outside people's immediate concerns may be much the same today as it always has been. What seems fairly clear is that large numbers of articulate people who have had much formal education and who often are opinion-formers exhibit an extremely low level of reflection. They readily espouse contradictory notions, some of which also run counter to the evidence of their own senses.[10]

Various explanations have been offered for the prevailing lack of reflection, which, as we have seen, often extends to an inability or reluctance to trust the obvious evidence of one's senses: the disturbing effects of very rapid scientific, technical, social and economic change; the erosion of traditional mores and modes of conduct; the bewildering effect of the multiplicity of concerns of people, and of the volume of diverse messages with which they are bombarded; and their reluctance to reflect on public issues which they are powerless to influence, including those which affect their personal well-being.

The prevailing bewilderment may owe something to the manifest failure of rapid material progress since the war to bring about the happiness or even contentment confidently expected of it. The post-war era has been one of unprecedented material prosperity, and in the 1950s and 1960s it was not yet marred by the anxieties attendant on inflation and on the various restrictions on movement between places and jobs. Yet the results of prosperity did not live up to the high hopes placed upon them.

These are speculative explanations for a baffling situation. I may add a further, possibly even more speculative, explanation, namely the decline of religious belief and of the authority of formal religion. The term itself derives from the Latin *religare*, to bind together. The decline in religion may well have affected the ability and readiness of people to think about things and relationships in a sustained and connected manner, especially when these fall outside their immediate experience or do not impinge upon their professional concerns.

Paradoxically, both believer and sceptic may be able to accept this explanation. A believer may argue that religious faith is necessary for a coherent view of the world, and that its decline undermines connected thinking all round. Conversely, a sceptic may maintain that religious faith helpfully concentrates human credulity into one area, and that its evaporation lets credulity loose in all directions.

6

When I first encountered economics it was a limited subject with a distinct core and circumscribed boundaries, both of which were recognized and accepted by the great majority of practitioners. Economists expected that their subject would progress and that it would make modest contributions to human well-being. The claims and ambitions were limited. In the course of its expansion since the mid-1930s, the subject has changed out of all recognition. The coincidence of impressive advances and of evident retrogression suggests that the recent expansion represents a pronounced watershed in economics. The subject has expanded in a number of different, indeed disparate, directions. Prominent economists are sometimes surprisingly unfamiliar with what once was the core of the subject. Even the mainstream of the subject is disfigured by crude transgressions. There are now many more academic economists than before the war, many of whom are much more prosperous than were their predecessors; and they cut more of a figure in the world. At the same time, many of them disregard the basics of their discipline, or are unfamiliar with simple economic realities.

The Spanish essayist, Ortega y Gasset, considered an absence of standards to be the essence of barbarism. 'Barbarism is the absence of standards to which appeal can be made.'[11] Conditions of barbarism in this sense have come to disfigure large tracts of modern economics.

163

Notes and References

Chapter 1
Remembrance of Studies Past: Retracing First Steps

1 The results of my studies are to be found in the following publications: *The Rubber Industry*, London and Cambridge, Mass., 1948; *Report on a Visit to the Rubber-Growing Small-holdings of Malaya*, London, 1948; *West African Trade*, Cambridge, 1954 and London, 1963; *Economic Analysis and Policy in Underdeveloped Countries*, Durham, NC, 1957, and Cambridge, 1958; *The Economics of Underdeveloped Countries* (with B. S. Yamey), London and Chicago, 1957; and some of the essays in *Markets, Market Control and Marketing Reform* (with B. S. Yamey), London, 1968.

2 In addition to what I have said in the Preface, I want to make it amply clear that as I have worked so closely with Basil Yamey since 1951, the ideas in this chapter are his as much as mine. It is for convenience of exposition alone that I do not make distinction in the text between our joint work and my own.

3 The plantation rubber industry comprises smallholdings, that is properties of less than 100 acres each, and estate properties of more than 100 acres each. Smallholdings which account for well over half the total area are entirely in Asian ownership. By now well over half of the estates are also in Asian, largely Chinese, ownership. In a private communication in January 1983, Mr W. G. G. Kellett, who was for many years Chief Statistician of the International Rubber Regulation Committee and subsequently of the International Rubber Study Group, put the present Asian ownership at well over 90 per cent.

4 The distinction between cultivable and uncultivable land is arbitrary. Adam Smith already noted that grapes could be grown in Scotland. The arbitrary nature of the distinction is highlighted by the experience of areas such as Holland, Venice, Israel and other Middle Eastern countries.

5 As I have observed in other places, these growth models have been inspired by Keynes' *General Theory*. He wrote there (p. 245):

'We take as given the existing skill and quantity of available labour, the existing quality and quantity of available equipment, the existing technique, the degree of competition, the tastes and habits of the consumer, and disutility of different intensities of labour and of the activities of supervision and organization, as well as the social structure. . . .

164

This drastic simplification is doubtfully appropriate even for the analysis of short-term growth in an advanced economy. It is altogether inappropriate to discussion of the long-term progress of ldcs.'

6 I use the past tense here to accord with the purpose of the World Bank's Pioneer Lecture series. As indicated in the Preface, this chapter is based on the original material of my lecture in that series.

7 W. Elkan *et al.*, 'The Economics of Shoe Shining in Nairobi', in *African Affairs*, Vol. 81, April 1982.

8 It is difficult to explain, in retrospect, why it was almost universally accepted as axiomatic in the early development economics that co-operative enterprises had such particular economic virtues that they should enjoy extensive state support and protection. A co-operative society is simply a form of economic organization. As such it does not inherently have access to sources of superior efficiency as compared with other types of organization, private or public. If co-operative societies had such attributes, they would not have needed official favours conferred on them.

9 Cf. 'The Economics of Marketing Reform', in P. T. Bauer and B. S. Yamey, *Markets, Market Control and Marketing Reform*, London, 1968.

10 When I first published my findings they were received with indignation by official spokesmen and by fellow economists. As late as the mid-1950s, the supporters of the Marketing Boards argued that the Boards were engaged only in price stabilization. By the 1960s it was generally accepted that they were and had been all along instruments of taxation. It is now also generally agreed that the proceeds of this taxation were in large measure wasted. The Marketing Boards were to a considerable extent descended from largely unsuccessful private produce-buying cartels; state monopsonies were introduced at the instigation of members of these cartels. Cf. Chapter 6 of this book.

11 Milton Friedman, 'The Reduction of Fluctuations in the Incomes of Primary Producers: A Critical Comment', in *Economic Journal*, Vol. 64, December 1954.

Chapter 2
Market Order and State Planning in Economic Development

1 For instance, in 1970 I lectured at a dozen or so Indian universities and research centres. At every one of them teachers and students took it for granted that central planning was indispensable for raising living standards. They insisted that the only question was to decide between Soviet and Chinese models of development. No one entertained the idea that the market system or personal choice could play a significant role.

2 *Development and Underdevelopment*, Cairo, 1956, p. 65. Emphasis as in the original.

3 *An International Economy*, London, 1956, p. 201.

4 H. Kitamura, 'Foreign Trade Problems in Planned Economic Development', in Kenneth Berrill (ed.), *Economic Development with Special Reference to East Asia*, London, 1963, p. 202. This passage and the one preceding it have been quoted by me in *Dissent on Development*, London and Cambridge, Mass., 1972, 1976, Chapter 6, where I discussed their significance and implications at greater length than here.

5 The case for replacing the market by centrally-planned economies is sometimes made to turn on the supposed need for large-scale taxation to finance development or to promote state-sponsored industrialization. I have examined some of these arguments in detail in *Dissent on Development*, London and Cambridge, Mass., 1972, 1976, especially in the Appendix to Chapter 2; and also in *Equality, the Third World and Economic Delusion*, London and Cambridge, Mass., 1981, especially Chapter 14.

6 For instance, Fawsey Mansour, 'Economic Cooperation Among Third World Countries –

Guidelines for a Charter', in *International Development Review*, 1970, No. 2.

7 Paul A. Baran, *The Political Economy of Growth*, New York, 1957, p. 177. In Chapter 10, below, I consider further the implications of this passage and of Baran's standing in the subject.

8 W. Arthur Lewis, *The Theory of Economic Growth*, Homewood, Illinois, 1955, p. 420.

9 I may mention a small picturesque example from West Africa of unexpected economic relationships and responses. In Southern Nigeria many people eat sun-dried fish. Almost the whole supply comes (or at least came until recently) from two sources. The first is the Arctic region of northern Norway and the second the inland lakes and rivers of the Chad region. Both are areas where a very dry atmosphere and a strong sun make possible the production of sun-dried fish of high keeping-quality. Northern Norway is about 6,000 miles away and the Chad region about 1,000 miles away from the principal areas of consumption. The consumers have repeatedly refused fish from other sources.

10 It is sometimes said to be a merit of planned economies that they have abolished unemployment. In fact unemployment and under-employment are virtually endemic in most of these economies.

11 Specific examples of the operation of some controls and of the tensions they generate are presented in detail in Chapter 6 below.

Chapter 3
Foreign Aid: Issues and Implications

1 *New York Times*, 1 March 1981.

2 As noted in the Preface, throughout this chapter foreign aid refers to official economic aid. It thus excludes military aid, private investment and the efforts of Western charities.

3 If the People's Republic of China is included in the South, as in the Brandt Report, the South has about four-fifths of the world's population. If China is excluded from both South and North, the former accounts for about two-thirds of the relevant total.

4 *North–South: A Programme for Survival* London, 1980, p. 262. See also Mahbub ul Haq, *The Poverty Curtain: Choice for the Third World*, New York, 1976, p. 181.

5 Three relatively recent arguments for aid (population explosion, oil prices and the international financial crisis) are examined briefly in section 12.

6 According to Kuznets, the contribution of the increases in material capital (both reproducible and non-reproducible) to the increase of *per capita* income over long periods in major developed countries ranged 'from less than a seventh to not much more than a fifth'. S. Kuznets, *Postwar Economic Growth*, Cambridge, Mass., 1964, p. 41. Much more important were improved efficiency in the use of resources and the movement of resources from less productive to more productive sectors.

7 The relation between investment and development is considered at greater length in P. T. Bauer, *Dissent on Development*, London and Cambridge, Mass., 1972, 1976, Chapter 2, and P. T. Bauer, *Equality, the Third World and Economic Delusion*, London and Cambridge, Mass., 1981, Chapter 14.

8 For the sake of formal completeness only, we note an exception to this proposition, even though it does not bear on the supply of development finance as normally discussed. Where the political survival of a newly-created country is widely doubted, it may not be able to raise capital even if it can use capital productively. This apparent exception to the rule that development does not depend on external aid is plainly irrelevant to the case for global transfers to the Third World.

9 Calculated from statistics in *Development Cooperation Review 1981*, OECD, Paris, 1982, and in *International Financial Statistics 1982 Yearbook*, International Monetary Fund, 1982.

10 A rough estimate suggests that currently foreign aid constitutes not more than 5 per cent of investment in the Third World. According to statistics in the World Bank's *World Development Report 1982*, all external finance was about 13 per cent of total investment in developing countries and foreign aid is about one-third of all external finance. If investment is taken to be about one-fifth of recorded GNP in the Third World, it follows that aid is about one per cent of recorded GNP (which materially understates actual GNP).

11 *World Development Report 1981*, The World Bank, Washington D.C., p. 58.

12 Deepak Lal, 'Debates on Development', unpublished manuscript, July 1982, pp. 73–5. Lal gives numerous references.

13 *World Bank Annual Report 1982*, Washington D.C., p. 25.

14 It is often urged that the deterioration in the commodity terms of trade of a number of Third World countries in the early 1980s has made it impossible for them to service their debts without intolerable hardship, if at all. Large-scale debt cancellation with or without further aid is said to be required to avert widespread distress or open default by Third World governments. This argument neglects major pertinent considerations. (i) Regardless of the deterioration of the commodity terms of some ldcs in the last year or two, the real burden of the bulk of Third World indebtedness has been much reduced by the general rise in prices since it was contracted, and also by various cancellations and postponements. (ii) As noted in the text, much of the debt was on concessionary, often highly concessionary, terms. (iii) Moreover, the debt service difficulties go back to the 1960s and 1970s when the terms of trade of the Third World generally were very favourable; the difficulties were experienced then and also subsequently by relatively prosperous countries such as the Argentine, Brazil, Chile, Ghana, Mexico and Turkey. Some of the poorest countries and societies, especially in Asia and Africa, have no external debts. (iv) Finally, governments acting responsibly can be expected to set aside reserves in periods of prosperity against the risk of a decline in the economic fortunes of their countries.

15 Werner Abelshauser, 'West German Economic Recovery, 1945–1951: a Reassessment', *Three Banks Review*, September 1982: '. . . foreign aid did not prove to be the crucial instrument in priming the German economy' (p. 35); '. . . foreign aid was not crucial in starting the recovery or in keeping it going' (p. 52).

16 Governments 'genuinely committed to improving the material standards of life of the mass of their population' are 'rare in the Third World'. C. H. Kirkpatrick and F. I. Nixson, 'The North–South Debate: Reflections on the Brandt Commission Report', in *Three Banks Review*, London, September 1981, p. 39.

17 The decision to build a new capital from scratch in the centre of Nigeria was based on political rather than social or economic grounds. The advocates of the construction of this new capital argued that it would help to unify the huge and heterogeneous country. In fact, instead of unifying the country, the project has already proved to be highly divisive. Critics complain that $9 billion has been spent to date 'and that much of this has vanished without producing visible results'; as yet 'the new capital . . . exists only on paper'. *The Economist*, London, 3–9 October 1981, p. 56. It is reported that expenditures of about $20 billion have been budgeted for Abuja. *Süddeutsche Zeitung*, 22 September 1981.

18 An officer of the government agency in charge of 'transforming Dodoma from a semi arid railway crossroads to an elegantly planned headquarters for the nation' said recently: 'I believe Dodoma is rapidly approaching a crisis. It will have to be abandoned or else saved by a major international rescue operation.' An Australian aid official who serves as information director and business manager for the new capital was reported as saying:

'Even if the project were given more money, I doubt whether it could all be spent. We cannot get enough cement, enough steel, enough diesel to run the trucks. But it is not only a question of financial resources and building materials, the country basically does not have

enough skilled people to properly run the place.'
The Times, London, 23 December 1981.
19 Even where aid is not earmarked by the donor for such specific projects, its receipt releases government funds for them.
20 This is an official estimate published by the Ministry for Economic Co-operation of the Federal Republic of Germany (in effect, the German Ministry for Foreign Aid), Bundesministerium für wirtschaftliche Zusammenarbeit, *Journalisten-Handbuch; Entwicklungspolitik*, Bonn, 1982, p. 201.
21 Indonesia is a routine recipient of Western aid.

'Indonesia's Liem family is well on the way to taking control of Hibernia Bank of San Francisco, the twelfth largest banking group in California. Via their Hong Kong interests, they plan to use the acquisition as a stepping-stone to further expansion, possibly in Europe.'

The Financial Times, London, 23 November 1982.
22 A more detailed account of this episode is presented in P. T. Bauer, *Equality, The Third World and Economic Delusion*, London and Cambridge, Mass., 1981, Chapter 5, pp. 113–14.
23 *Kinderfibel: Ein Bilderbuch zum Mitdenken*, Bundesministerium für wirtschaftliche Zusammenarbeit, Bonn, 1982, p. 30. The sentence in the original is 'Gleich viel für jeden – so muss es werden.'
24 If the Atlantic slave trade called for restitution now, much of this should be logically from the African states to the United States, Brazil and some Caribbean countries where live the descendants of the slaves who were the victims of this trade. The beneficiaries were the African captors and sellers of slaves, and their buyers and owners in the West.
   Except over very short periods, at most a generation or two, historical wrongs cannot be rectified. For instance, in practice it is not possible to identify the descendants of perpetrators, beneficiaries and victims of these wrongs. And how far should we go back in time to rectify these wrongs? Should the Soviet Union pay reparations to Iraq and Syria for the destruction brought about there by the Mongols in the thirteenth century (who came from the regions which are now Soviet Central Asia)? Should Britain pay a restitution to France for the ravages inflicted by English troops (many the descendants of Normans) and their Burgundian allies?
25 For a detailed discussion of population and economic development, see Chapter 3 of P. T. Bauer, *Equality, the Third World and Economic Delusion*.
26 Professor Harold Rose has suggested that prediction of prospective new arguments for aid would make an interesting quasi-academic parlour game. At present (November 1982), candidates would include reparation for misguided advice by Western donors in the past (this is beginning to surface), or for the effects of Western trade barriers. Damaging effects of price changes are an evergreen which can always be used afresh, and can confidently be expected to remain or reappear on the menu. The prices of traded goods change frequently and most ldcs both import and export various commodities, so that aid can always be urged as necessary to compensate some importing or exporting country.
27 *IDA in Retrospect*, World Bank, Washington D.C., 1982, p. xiv.
28 Commodity schemes as a form of aid are examined in P. T. Bauer, *Equality, the Third World and Economic Delusion*, London and Cambridge, Mass., 1981, Chapter 8.
29 The relevant statistics will be found in a publication by the Organization for Economic Co-operation and Development, *Development Cooperation: 1980 Review*, Paris, 1980, p. 103.
30 *North–South: A Programme for Survival*, London, 1980, pp. 290–1.

Chapter 4
Multinational Aid: An Improvement?

1 *Partners in Development: Report of the Commission on International Development*, London, 1969, p. 214.
2 Ibid.
3 *IDA in Retrospect*, published for the World Bank, Washington D.C., 1982, p. 79.
4 According to *Development Cooperation: 1980 Review*, OECD, 1981:

> 'For the coming years Germany has announced its intention of increasing aid appropriations at a rate twice as fast as that of the federal budget as a whole.'

This was agreed by all three political parties at a time when budgetary problems were a source of intense inter-party conflict. Some of the fiscal economies proposed in 1980–2 were politically highly sensitive and extremely unpopular. These included the elimination of the transport subsidies to and from West Berlin, reduction in the general financial support to that city, and cuts in federal welfare spending, including family allowances. The sums involved in some of these were trivial compared to foreign aid: the saving through the elimination of the transport subsidies, which jeopardized some of these services, was two per cent of the spending on aid. Conflicts over these economies and over the proposed increase in Value Added Tax brought about the break-up of the ruling coalition. But all parties were agreed throughout that foreign aid should be increased. This unanimous support for aid was particularly noteworthy in that the great bulk of German aid to the less developed world was untied.
5 'Britain reluctantly agreed yesterday to make a contribution of up to 1m dollars to Argentina over the next few years for its development. The money represents Britain's share of a 20m dollar credit proposed by the United Nations Development Programme (UNDP) . . . British objections to any aid for Argentina had caused the Chairman of the Council to delay the debate on the project. No vote was taken. British officials said later that they would have voted against the credit for Argentina, but that the rules of UNDP meant that they could only delay the credit by a week.'
The Financial Times, London, 5 June 1982.
6 It was reported that the Director General himself administered the disposal of a large fund. The objects of expenditure did not have to be listed publicly. It appears that a large number of small countries were the beneficiaries of the fund. It was suggested that this served to strengthen his personal position. The Director General had been appointed in 1976 under provisions calling for a one-time six-year term. He 'soon engineered a change in the rules to permit a second term'. *International Herald Tribune*, 10 November 1981. He has since been reappointed.
7 France, Italy, Australia and Austria voted for the budget. The position of France reflected its political and economic interests in Francophone Africa, a special beneficiary of FAO funds. Australia was concerned to secure the appointment to the vacant post of Director of the World Food Programme, with the support of Dr Saouma, the FAO Director General. *Neue Zürcher Zeitung*, 28 November 1981. Austria supported the budget proposals, and also the rejection of external assessments, on the ground that there was no need for independent scrutiny as long as recipient countries were satisfied. Italy's support for the budget proposals as well as for the FAO itself needs no explanation.
8 The preceding account of the FAO budget conference is based on the sources already cited, and on a number of detailed reports and commentaries in the *Neue Zürcher Zeitung* and the *Frankfurter Allgemeine Zeitung*, between 6 October and 5 December 1981. Brief reports

169

are also in *The Financial Times*, 12 and 26 November 1981. The main elements in these accounts and commentaries are discernible in the FAO's published summary of the budget conference, *Report of the Conference of the FAO*, Rome, 1981, especially pp. 23, 25 and Appendix D.

9 *Commentary*, March 1975.

10 ' "We are actually poorer than we were in 1972", Dr Nyerere said last December'. *International Herald Tribune*, 23–4 October 1982.

11 *International Herald Tribune*, 23–4 October 1982. During the 1970s, publications by World Bank officials had drawn attention to the serious adverse effects of official policies in Tanzania.

12 *World Bank Atlas*, 1981, p. 6.

13 See, for example, J. Clark Leith, *Foreign Trade Regimes and Economic Development: Ghana*, New York, 1974, pp. 65 and 165; and *The Times*, London, 3 February 1983.

14 A more detailed discussion is to be found in P. T. Bauer, *Equality, The Third World and Economic Delusion*, London and Cambridge, Mass., 1981, Chapter 6.

15 The booklet *IDA in Retrospect*, published for the World Bank, New York, 1982, to which I have already referred, is a handsome document, with many useful statistics. Much of the text, however, is little more than self-congratulatory propaganda. The following passage (from p. 78) gives the flavour:

'In sum, IDA has been a very successful and very effective development institution. Its impact is difficult to judge because its accomplishments, while very real, are the outcome of processes and efforts of which IDA is only a part, often a small one. What can be said, however, is that in the face of the extremely difficult task entrusted to IDA, it has channelled its money prudently, for very useful and often vital purposes.'

Nothing is said about the policies of the governments whose resources have been augmented by IDA money, including the policies of the governments of India and Tanzania in the 1970s. The publication was released in August 1982. It specifically instances Mexico and Brazil among current contributors to IDA, and yet in August 1982 Mexico declared itself insolvent and precipitated the world banking crisis, which promptly came to be used as a further argument for multinational aid. Brazil is now another major problem debtor.

16 An example of the Western deference to the Third World comes from an altogether different context. A report in *The Times*, London, 3 January 1983, commented on a recent World Cup football competition. It attributed the shambles to the decision of the organizing committee 'who appointed 41 referees all from different countries exclusively on the basis of political appeasement of the Third World. . .'.

Chapter 5
Ecclesiastical Economics: Envy Legitimized

1 The numbers in parentheses in the text refer to the numbered paragraphs in these documents. The passages are quoted from the official English texts published by Polyglot Press, Vatican City, in 1967 and 1971. Unless stated otherwise, references to the Pope are to Paul VI. Some of the passages I quote incorporate statements from other prominent Catholic sources. As these statements are accepted and endorsed by the Pope, I shall usually not refer to the original sources but quote them as expressions of the Pope's views. The present Pope, John Paul II, seems to share the central opinions on economic matters of his recent predecessors. This is suggested by the encyclical *Laborem Exercens*, 1981, which is, however, less calculated to arouse envy and resentment than the encyclicals of Paul VI. I shall not on this occasion quote Protestant clergymen or theologians. Elsewhere I have

examined some opinions by Professor Ronald J. Sider, a prominent evangelical churchman, on the subject of economic differences between the West and the Third World. His opinions are typical of much contemporary evangelical thought. He is quoted extensively in the chapter entitled 'Western Guilt and Third World Poverty', in P. T. Bauer, *Equality, the Third World and Economic Delusion*, London and Cambridge, Mass., 1981.

2 The modishness, one might say trendiness, of the papal documents is evident throughout. Section headings include 'Women', 'Environment' and 'Development – A New Name for Peace'. The documents also, unsurprisingly, discuss such topics as debt rescheduling, commodity agreements and rent controls – in every instance at an amateur, populist level.

3 Quoted by Malcolm Deas, 'Catholics and Marxists', in *London Review of Books*, 19 March 1981.

4 Julius Nyerere, 'The Economic Challenge: Dialogue or Confrontation', in *African Affairs*, London, April 1976.

5 Quoted by Malcolm Deas, 'Catholics and Marxists', in *London Review of Books*, 19 March 1981.

6 Especially in the past, people have often acquired wealth not by peaceful economic contacts in commercial transactions, but by despoiling other people. Where there is no public security, the strong can despoil the weak so regularly that this is not even regarded as criminal. Such conditions may well have been widespread in the fourth century AD when St Ambrose denounced the rich (cf. section 3 above), though it is doubtful whether he specifically had in mind spoilation by the rich. The acquisition of wealth in this way does not, of course, represent the generation of income as this is usually understood. Moreover, spoliation results from lack of public security. Where a government fails to perform its primary function, it is extremely improbable that it would or could organize redistribution on any basis likely to be fair.

7 An extended discussion of redistribution within a country is in Chapter 1 of P. T. Bauer, *Equality, the Third World and Economic Delusion*, London and Cambridge, Mass., 1981.

8 Cf. Chapter 2, section 9, and Chapter 3, section 7, above.

Chapter 6
Black Africa: The Living Legacy of Dying Colonialism

1 These matters are more fully discussed in P. T. Bauer, *Equality, the Third World and Economic Delusion*, London and Cambridge, Mass., 1981, Chapter 9, section 5.

2 Joyce Cary, *Selected Essays*, 1976, pp. 85, 97, 100.

3 The colonial administrators sometimes used African chiefs in attempts to enforce unpopular measures and practices on agricultural producers. These usually ill-considered interventions helped to prejudice the position of the chiefs, and so to ease the way for the new nationalist politicians.

4 The riots in Accra in 1948 and in Enugu in 1949, in which many lives were lost and much property destroyed, were examples of inadequate maintenance of public security. In Lagos, in the summer of 1951, groups of strong-arm men openly flouted the law and manhandled people who wanted to work in defiance of an unofficial strike. At the same time the Nigerian government extended the system of export monopoly to include sunflower seed, a commodity so unimportant that it was not listed separately in most official trade statistics.

5 Obafemi Awolowo, *Path to Nigerian Freedom*, 1947, quoted in Sir Frederick Pedler, *Main Currents of West African History 1940–1978*, 1979 (italics added).

6 Somewhat similar sequences took place in other former African colonies. But in Francophone Africa at any rate, the changes were less abrupt, chiefly because more *dirigiste*

171

policies were pursued in these territories than in British Africa before the Second World War, and also because the new ruling groups were on the whole numerically less important than in the former British colonies.

The following passage comes from an unexpected source – *Development Co-operation: 1982 Review*, OECD, Paris, 1982, p. 17:

'Another heritage from their colonial eras seems to be a source of current difficulties, although it is seldom cited by African leaders; this is the colonial administrations' latter-day penchant for extensive economic controls and state monopolies. This precedent may have predisposed many new African governments, despite their very limited cadres of skilled administrators and analysts, to opt for state enterprises, especially in export and agriculture, and for controls on trade and investment, regulation of prices, and gambles on large-scale state-owned or state-subsidized development schemes.'

The author does not appreciate that the damaging effects of these policies do not depend upon the size and efficiency of the cadres.

7 A selection of these opinions by Mary Kingsley, A. McPhee and Sir Keith Hancock is quoted in P. T. Bauer, *Dissent on Development*, London and Cambridge, Mass., 2nd. ed., 1976, Chapter 1.

8 The official undertakings given to the British Parliament, that the Marketing Boards would not be used as instruments of taxation, were unusually explicit and specific. Thus a White Paper, Command 6950, 1946, stated:

'It will be apparent from the above description of the boards' proposed method of operation that there will be no question of their making a profit at the expense of West African cocoa producers . . . on the average of a period of years . . . the average price paid in West Africa will be substantially equal to the average net price realized on world markets, and the boards' buying and selling transactions will, therefore, approximately balance.'

9 A letter in *The Times*, London, 20 July 1951, by 'Your Correspondent recently in Nigeria' (in fact Oliver Woods, the newspaper's Colonial Editor) supported the persistent underpayment of farmers, on the ground that it prevented the emergence of kulaks in Nigeria.

10 These effects were foreseen by the late H. S. Booker, lecturer at the London School of Economics, who was at the time on secondment to the Gold Coast government as Assistant Census Commissioner. He predicted that unless the import cuts were rescinded, or fiscal measures taken to reduce consumer demand, the tensions in the winter of 1948 would be so acute as to bring about civil disturbance. For saying this publicly he was dismissed from his post and indeed virtually deported. His predictions were fulfilled to the letter.

11 The principal events which we have summarized here are described in published documents, though some of these are not easily available outside West Africa. (For instance, the Sachs Report, which was published in the Gold Coast, received only a very limited circulation.) It was possible to fill out some of the details from other sources, principally the files of the Colonial Office and the Gold Coast Secretariat, and also from interviews with civil servants and the leading merchant firms.

12 It is often thought that the attempted secession of Biafra from Nigeria was prompted by the prospects of large oil revenues. However, the extensive politicization of economic life in Nigeria, the resulting political tension, the killings of Ibo in the north, and the demands for secession all antedated the prospects of large oil revenues.

13 I may observe here an incidental by-product of the operation of the state export monopolies. The Marketing Boards first drew some of the most influential *dirigiste* economists into the affairs of the Third World. In widely publicized articles these academics supported the Marketing Boards, in particular the heavy under-payment of the producers.

This support helped to bring about the alliance between *dirigiste* economists, journalists and civil servants, which has done so much to shape Western attitudes and conduct towards the Third World.

14 Kleptocracy is the term coined by Professor S. L. Andreski of Reading University to denote polities whose governance is pervaded by corruption and extortion.

Chapter 7
Industrialization and Development: The Nigerian Experience

1 Peter Kilby, *Industrialization in an Open Economy: Nigeria 1945–1966*, Cambridge, England, 1969, pp. xii and 399.

2 It is unfortunate that Professor Kilby has restricted his discussion of processing for export so largely to palm oil. There is in Nigeria a substantial groundnut processing industry which was established in the 1940s in the face of persistent official opposition, especially by the Groundnut Marketing Board. The opposition of the Nigerian Groundnut Marketing Board to processing is discussed in P. T. Bauer, *West African Trade*, Cambridge, 1954, Appendix 4. In his short discussion of groundnut processing, Kilby writes that after 1961 'competitive pressures in the inter-regional race to industrialize' were responsible for a more encouraging attitude to the establishment and expansion of groundnut crushing (p. 171).

3 The improvement in the physical quality of palm oil exports does not necessarily reflect an economic improvement. The identification of the two concepts rests on a confusion between technical and economic efficiency, a confusion which in turn reflects a disregard of the relevance of costs and prices. This issue is examined in P. T. Bauer and B. S. Yamey, 'The Economics of Marketing Reform', *Journal of Political Economy*, LXII, June 1954, reprinted in our book, *Markets, Market Control and Marketing Reform*, London 1968.

4 Kilby provides yet another illustration of this general point. He shows that the heavy protection of the textile industry in Nigeria involved a greater drain on foreign exchange than it saved through substitution for imports. 'All evidence suggests that the foreign exchange cost of domestically produced cloth is greater than that of imported cloth. . . . In the most unfavourable and increasingly important case of printing on imported cloth, the cost of the imported raw materials alone exceeds the value of the imports being replaced' (p. 126).

5 Kilby adds that 'by causing a diversion of potential investment resources to consumption', the raising of wage rates 'may have slowed the rate of economic growth'. His tentative conclusion here may reflect his clear recognition that there is no simple relation between investment and growth, and the knowledge that a large part of public-sector investment in industry in Nigeria has had negative returns. On the first point, Kilby writes in a brief historical survey in Chapter 1: 'Nigeria's performance well illustrates that aggregate investment does not cause economic growth, nor can it even be correlated in developing economies with advances in real output, given that non market-directed public investment represents a significant share in total investment' (p. 10).

6 Kilby's recognition of the problems and difficulties should have made him more sceptical than he appears to be of the contribution which could be made by foreign specialists to the improvement in the 'quality of policy formulation' by government in Nigeria (p. 363). He also appears too sanguine about the contribution to applied industrial research for Nigeria to be expected from foreign graduates financed and recruited by UNESCO, AID and the Ford Foundation (p. 198).

7 This uncritical approach to statistics is of course not confined to the development literature. In the West also, statistics are only too often made to bear a burden which they cannot sustain, especially when they are made to serve as basis for policy.

8 Excellent discussions of some of these problems will be found in various writings by

173

Professor Dan Usher, especially *The Price Mechanism and the Meaning of National Income Statistics*, Oxford, 1968.

9 As an illustration of such a transfer, Kilby instances the cigarette industry's efforts to improve the production of tobacco in Nigeria.

10 We may note here that the term industrialization as used in much of the development literature is ambiguous in that it denotes different situations or processes in which three elements are present in different proportions: the growth of manufacturing, which often but not invariably accompanies certain stages of material advance; modernization of attitudes, institutions and economic processes; and the state support of manufacturing. The components or elements are often present simultaneously, but they are distinct. The most frequent use of the term interprets it in the third of these senses, that is state-sponsored or subsidized manufacturing. Kilby employs industrialization in this sense, with some elements of the first use of the term.

11 Income elasticity of demand denotes the responsiveness of demand to changes in income; it is expressed as the ratio of the proportionate change in quantity demanded to the proportionate change in income associated with it. A low income elasticity of demand, that is one of a numerical value of less than unity, is often confused in the literature with a negative income elasticity of demand, that is one with a value of less than zero.

12 A succinct yet comprehensive critical review of the arguments for subsidized industrialization in less developed countries will be found in Harry G. Johnson, 'Commercial Policy and Industrialization', a lecture delivered at the University of Panama, 12 August 1971, and published in *Economica*, 1972, xxxix. These arguments are discussed at greater length in P. T. Bauer, *Dissent on Development*, London and Cambridge, Mass., 1972, 1976, Chapters 2 and 6.

Chapter 8
The Economics of Post-War Immigration Policy in British West Africa

1 In Nigeria the immigration ordinance is Chapter 89 of 1947; in the Gold Coast it is Ordinance No. 7 of 1947.

2 Trade in technical goods and equipment is an exception. It is officially recognized that Africans to some extent lack the necessary skills and capital required in these trades.

3 Levantines include Lebanese, Syrians, Greeks, Cypriots and Arabs. Lebanese are the most numerous in West Africa.

4 Control of the immigration of technical personnel is less rigorous.

5 In 1948, the firm of John Holt and Company printed for private circulation the very interesting diary of the founder of the firm, *The Diary of John Holt*. The publication provides a vivid account of the formative years of this well-known West African enterprise. It is also a case-study which illustrates many of the points made in the analysis and discussion in this chapter. It is of special interest that most of the ways in which the founder of the firm, John Holt, built up the present vast enterprise would today either be barred by immigration control or be hedged about with crippling restrictions. Indeed, they would fall foul of the basic assumptions and principles of the present immigration policy.

The first John Holt went out to West Africa as a clerk, storekeeper and foreman in the employ of the British consul at Fernando Po, who was a trader and had two shops and a farm. After the death of the owner, the small trading enterprise was managed for some time for his widow by John Holt, who later bought it from her out of his own savings and began to trade on his own account. Most of his trade was of a type which today would be regarded as retail trade. Eventually he became the founder of a highly respected enterprise, which is now one of the foremost firms of direct importers in West Africa. Its activities include the operation of a shipping line and a river fleet, and it controls or is associated with several manufacturing enterprises.

6 In practice, the control of immigration tends to favour the established trading firms, especially the large ones, in several other ways as well. The limitation on the number of expatriate employees is less onerous for the large firms than for the smaller ones. A large firm can discontinue particular activities and release labour for more profitable or important tasks, while a small firm has less room for manoeuvre. Again, the entry of people with some kind of formal technical qualification is less severely restricted than that of mercantile employees. Large firms with technical departments can often make other use of their technical personnel. Moreover, the established firms are better known to the administrations and more familiar with local administrative practices. They are thus able to draft and present their applications for additional staff more effectively than newcomers. Levantine firms find it especially difficult to obtain permission to augment their expatriate staff.

7 W. K. Hancock, *Survey of British Commonwealth Affairs*, Part II, Vol. II, Chapter II, *passim*.

8 The maintenance of British personnel in West Africa is expensive. The Managing Director of the United Africa Company estimated in 1950 that it cost his company over £1,400 a year to employ and maintain the most junior European employee in West Africa. The cost of employing and maintaining a Levantine was certainly much lower, very likely less than half this figure. New enterprises cannot afford to carry such costly personnel in the early stages. Their commercial prospects would be improved if they were able to employ less expensive Levantines.

9 The competitive relationship between certain groups and participants in economic life is apt to be perceived more readily than is the complementary (or mutually beneficial) relationship. The reaction noted in the text is an example.

10 Some of the Africans who may benefit in the short run probably lose part or all of the benefits if the long-run effects of the restrictions on the growth of the economy are included in the calculation.

11 It might perhaps be possible to devise a politically acceptable system under which a somewhat larger number of expatriates could be admitted than at present, for a stated number of years (which would, however, have to be over ten years to make fixed investment by the individuals concerned worthwhile), without definite expectation either of extension beyond that period or of the granting of political rights. If such a scheme were politically acceptable, it might contribute substantially to economic development.

Chapter 9
Substance and Method in Development Economics: A Commentary on the Views of Professor Stern

1 Nicholas H. Stern, 'Professor Bauer on Development', in *Journal of Development Economics*, Vol. 1, 1974, pp. 191–211. Unless otherwise indicated, references are to Stern's article or to my book *Dissent on Development*, London and Cambridge, Mass., 1972, 1976, to parts of which Stern's article is addressed.

2 I specified this model in detail and then summarized it: 'The model behind the thesis of the vicious circle of poverty pivots on the notion that the low level of income itself prevents the capital formation required to raise income' (p. 33).

3 The rapid material progress of a number of ldcs with low *per capita* incomes has been noted by many writers. Here is an example: 'We hear a lot about the relative stagnation of those

parts of Africa which are on the fringes of the desert. Not many people know that some of the fastest growing countries in the world are in what is called "Black Africa" (to distinguish the centre from both North and South)' (W. A. Lewis, *Aspects of Tropical Trade, 1883–1965*, Stockholm, 1969, p. 15). The substantial growth of many ldcs has now become a familiar theme of the literature, although it is usually combined with complaints about the insufficient benefit to the poorest countries and groups; cf., for instance, H. B. Chenery *et al.*, *Redistribution with Growth*, Oxford, 1974.

4 I note two specific points in passing. First, Stern writes (p. 198): 'It must be admitted that the authors cited by Bauer were vague but it is rather unfair to pick a few observations from a period after the one they were discussing.' Examination of the pages of my book (pp. 452–3) referred to by Stern shows the following. The quotation from Myrdal refers explicitly to the continuing present, not to the last fifty or a hundred years as suggested by Stern. Moreover, the reference on these pages to Singer and Rosenstein-Rodan simply makes the point that they do not produce any evidence for the period they are writing about. Second, on the question of relative income levels and absolute income levels, Stern writes: 'The issue is much more open than Bauer grants – it is an ethical question and there is no monopoly on the truth' (p. 198). Reference to my book on the page cited (p. 51) will show that I merely pointed to the difference between the two concepts, and to the fact that the corresponding indices often move in different directions. I noted further that in most contexts the relative concept is the one usually regarded as interesting or pertinent. I did not close the issue or pontificate on the matter.

5 Usher has examined these matters very closely. He has argued on the basis of detailed observation and analysis that the biases and errors of income estimates in ldcs often amount to several hundred per cent. Stern writes in a footnote (p. 204) that 'Usher's recalculations for the United Kingdom and Thailand, while narrowing the gap considerably, still leave large income differences (over 3:1 in 1963)' (1963 should read 1958). He does not tell his readers that Usher wrote: 'For example, the conventional comparison shows that the *per capita* national income of the United Kingdom is about fourteen times that of Thailand.' *Economica*, May 1963, p. 140. Thus Usher's recomputations reduce the ratio of incomes by four hundred per cent, a fact which is not clear from Stern's reference.

6 The arbitrariness of the dividing line between dcs and ldcs on the basis of income is underlined further by the presence of substantial group and regional differences in incomes within particular countries. *Per capita* incomes of regions and groups in many ldcs are often higher than incomes in rich countries, and even more than those of substantial groups and regions there.

7 Although the phenomenon of economic decline, whether relative or absolute, is rarely noted in development economics, it is pertinent in many contexts including the ideas of cumulative causation and of the widening gap. The obvious pertinence, now ignored, was recognized 2,500 years ago, as can be seen in the following quotation:

'For most cities which were great once are small today; and those which used to be small were great in my own time. Knowing, therefore, that human prosperity never abides long in the same place, I shall pay attention to both alike.' [Herodotus, *The Histories*, Book 1.]

8 Changes in life expectation, and their implications, are discussed fully in P. T. Bauer, *Dissent on Development*, Chapter 1, and P. T. Bauer, *Equality, The Third World and Economic Delusion*, Chapter 3.

9 For further discussion of this major issue, see Chapter 3, above, and also P. T. Bauer, *Equality, The Third World and Economic Delusion*, Chapter 1.

10 Stern himself writes (p. 201):

'There may also be objectives distinct from the size of the national income and its distribution. For example, a desire for collective decision-making will have consequences for views on decentralization through the price mechanism. These alternative objectives are perfectly legitimate, have implications for government intervention and are ignored by Bauer.'

I ignored the 'desire for collective decision-making' because, as I made clear, I was concerned with the effects of planning on living standards and because, in ldcs, proponents of central planning almost invariably claim that it is necessary for the improvement of living standards. Moreover, it makes little sense to imply that in some ldcs central planning may reflect a 'desire for collective decision-making'. Who shares the desire? How is the preference declared? And in what sense, other than that of political rhetoric, does central planning as it is practised involve collective decision-making? Finally, on Stern's argument, any supposed preference for governmental action would provide its own justification.

11 In two publications (*The Rubber Industry*, London, 1948, and *Report on a Visit to Rubber Growing Smallholdings of Malaya*, London, 1948) I proposed state intervention in the establishment of new capacity of smallholders' rubber by forest clearing and new planting, and in the organization of marketing of smallholders' rubber, on grounds somewhat similar to those noted by Stern. After observation of subsequent developments in East and West Africa, South Asia and South-East Asia, including the extensive politicization of economic life, I would not now put forward such proposals.

12 Pearce has written in a similar vein in the context of international trade theory and policy that 'much of the writing in this field proceeds on the argument that government is carried on not by a group of elected politicians vainly trying to please everybody, but by a highly trained executive armed with more detailed information than it can possibly have, consciously seeking a perfect tax-subsidy system, designed to give effect at all times to Adam Smith's rule and to no other' (I. F. Pearce, 'The death of laissez faire', in *The Times Literary Supplement*, London, 7 February 1975, p. 144). I note here two studies based on detailed examination of the relative economic success of more and less closely-planned economies: H. Myint, *Economic Theory and the Underdeveloped Countries*, London, 1971; and S. Wellisz, 'Lessons of twenty years of planning in developing countries', in *Economica*, Vol. 38, 1971.

13 I also noted that there are poor societies and countries which did not register much material progress in recent decades, but that these instances do not validate the hypothesis of the vicious circle (p. 41).

14 As noted repeatedly in my book, it was recognition of this difficulty which induced me in certain contexts to speculate on the reasons behind the espousal and acceptance of ideas, the invalidity of which should be immediately obvious. Such speculation has no bearing on the validity either of the argument or of the criticism. But readers, especially non-technical readers, may not believe that such ideas are being seriously advanced, and criticism may therefore gain in effectiveness by such reflections. It may be thought that such notions are no more than harmless aberrations. This is not so. Their propagation and acceptance are harmful not only intellectually but also in terms of practical policy. For instance, the notion of the vicious circle diverts attention from the prime determinants of development, from the possibilities of influencing them favourably, as well as from the many acute problems which result not from stagnation but from rapid and uneven change; the notion of the inevitability of payments difficulties in the course of development obscures the role of monetary and fiscal policy; and so on.

15 It is not obvious that 'total new resources' is the same as 'domestic production plus capital inflow'. This is merely one example of the looseness of exposition in much of Stern's article.

177

16 I may note one of Stern's points (p. 208): 'Low savings may cause a balance of payments deficit if it is insufficient to meet investment.' Stern shows no curiosity as to how this state of affairs is brought about. It simply happens, it seems, that there is some given volume of investment, that saving is deficient and that foreigners make resources available. Moreover, Stern does not consider whether the prospect of foreign aid might not cause a government to choose or induce a level of capital expenditure which makes inevitable a balance-of-payments deficit.

17 Stern refers twice on the same page (p. 208) to a paper by M. Lipton. The reader who is not familiar with that paper may be surprised to learn that the main conclusion of the relevant section is to cast serious doubt on the validity of the methods and hence findings of the then-available statistical studies of aid and growth. He may be further surprised to learn that Lipton's favourable conclusion on aid and growth ('opposite Bauer's own') is not based on statistical analysis, or even on discussion of examples which 'straddle the spectrum of possible examples' – the two methods favoured by Stern (p. 194). Indeed, Lipton's conclusion is based partly on the attempted demonstration that 'the statistical case against the effectiveness of aid is not proven', and partly on the claim that the 'common sense of 'more means more' can *in future* be powerfully reinforced by allocative measures to associate aid with an increasingly self-reliant path to growth and the relief of poverty' (M. Lipton, 'Aid allocation when aid is inadequate', in T. J. Byres (ed.), *Foreign Resources and Economic Development*, London, 1972, pp. 178–9, italics added).

18 D. Usher, *The Price Mechanism and the Meaning of National Income Statistics*, Oxford, 1968. Usher's observations have not been refuted; they have in fact been commended by Professors Phyllis Deane and Paul Samuelson, among others.

19 'We shall produce any statistics that we think will help us to get as much money out of the United States as we possibly can. Statistics which we do not have, but which we need to justify our demands, we will simply fabricate.' O. Morgenstern, *On the Accuracy of Economic Observations*, London, 2nd ed., 1963, p. 21, quoting an unnamed civil servant whose statement Morgenstern clearly believes to be apposite.

20 To avoid misunderstanding, it seems necessary to state that for certain specific purposes not involving international or inter-temporal comparisons, estimates of the flow of incomes in the exchange sector of ldcs can be very useful. But this is different from the issues discussed by Stern in the above context.

Chapter 10
Further Reflections on the State of Economics

1 Gunnar Myrdal has been among those who have explicitly recognized the external influence on the ideas of economists. Cf. *The Political Element in the Development of Economic Theory*, London, 1953.

2 I have speculated on the reasons for these attitudes in Chapter 2, section 10, above, and in 'Western Guilt and Third World Poverty', in *Equality, The Third World and Economic Delusion*, London and Cambridge, Mass., 1981, Chapter 4.

3 This particular passage is quoted in P. T. Bauer, *Dissent on Development*, London and Cambridge, Mass., 1972, 1976, Chapter 4.

4 In 1979, the World Bank published a long study on Romania, according to which the Romanian economy grew at a rate of 9.8 per cent a year over the period 1950 to 1975. Taken together with the income at the end of the period surveyed in the report, this growth rate implied that at the beginning of the period, incomes must have been too low to sustain life. This was explained clearly in an article entitled 'The Resurrection of the Dead' in the *Wall Street Journal*, 10 August 1979. Another World Bank volume, *Twenty-five Years of*

Economic Development 1950 to 1975 by D. Morawetz, was published in 1977. It stated that, by the early 1970s, 'the evidence of China's remarkable success in development began to filter out to the rest of the world' (p. 9). Neither the evidence nor the criterion of success is examined in the book. By 1977 the hardships and failures of the policies under Mao Tse Tung, which had been evident for some time, were publicized by his successors.

5 The advocacy of state-supported industrialization, especially large-scale expansion of capital goods industries, has often proceeded without reference to prices, costs and demand, and also on the assumption that foreign exchange earnings are given and are independent of domestic demand and rates of exchange. As should be clear from simple economic analysis, foreign exchange earnings would be unaffected by domestic conditions and by exchange rates if, and only if, the elasticity of foreign demand for each tradeable good were exactly unity at every level of price. And this is inconceivable.

6 A further illustration of the type of inconsistency noted here is the coexistence in some of the development literature of the view that factor proportions are fixed in major branches of economic activity and the idea that multinational companies inflict capital-intensive technologies on ldcs inappropriate to their conditions, thereby aggravating unemployment.

7 Some critical comments by prominent academic economists on the state of their subject are set out in Chapter 15 of P. T. Bauer, *Equality, The Third World and Economic Delusion*, London and Cambridge, Mass., 1981.

8 'Those who are best fitted to guide the public opinion think it beneath them to expose mere nonsense, and comfort themselves by reflecting that such popularity cannot last. This contemptuous levity has been carried too far.'
Macaulay, 'Mr Robert Montgomery', in *Critical and Historical Essays*, London, 1923.

9 Understanding of economic and social reality has also been inhibited by an insufficiently critical adoption of methods which have proved highly effective in the natural sciences. The rapid and extensive application of some of these methods in the social sciences has tended to obscure rather than to inform. This tendency has been noted explicitly by scholars highly qualified in social science or the natural sciences, or both. Cf. P. T. Bauer, *Equality, The Third World and Economic Delusion*, London and Cambridge, Mass., 1981, Chapter 15, footnotes 9 to 13.

10 This observation again is not eccentric.

'It seems to me that we are living in a time of human sterility, reducing the whole of human experience to chaos so as to justify a deliberate, headlong flight from reason into the absurd. . . .'

Berthold Lubetkin in the course of his acceptance address on receiving the Royal Gold Medal of the Royal Institute of British Architects: *The Times*, London, 15 July 1982.

11 Ortega y Gasset, *The Revolt of the Masses*, London, 1932, p. 79.

Index

Aba, 110
Abelshauser, Werner, 167n
aborigines, 8, 39, 83
Abramovitz, Moses, 44
Abuja, 51, 167n
Accra riots, 103, 171n
advisers, economic, 153
Afghanistan, foreign aid, 56
agriculture: availability of land, 8; capital
  formation, 3, 10; cash crops, 2–4, 5, 14, 26, 91;
  export crops, 2–4; interaction with rest of
  Nigerian economy, 123–5; productivity, 8;
  restrictions on, 49; state controls, 35; state
  monopoly of exports, 93, 94–5, 96–100
aid, see foreign aid; multinational aid
aid education, 70
airlines, 46, 51
Algeria, armed conflict, 40
Ambrose, Saint, 74, 171n
Amin, President, 66
Andreski, S. L., 172n
Argentine: external debts, 167n; multinational aid,
  66, 169n
armed conflict, 40, 42–3
arms expenditure, 51
Association of West African Merchants (AWAM),
  97, 100–3
Australia: colonialism, 58; FAO budget, 169n
Austria, FAO budget, 169n
Awolowo, Obafemi, 171n

Bahrein, foreign aid, 42
balance of payments: foreign aid and, 55; ldcs and,
  113, 127
banks, foreign aid and, 60
Baran, Paul A., 22, 156–7, 166n
Barclays Bank, 97
Bauer, P. T., 164n, 165n, 166n 168nn, 170nn,
  171nn, 172n, 173n, 174n, 176nn, 178n, 179nn
Belize, armed conflict, 40
Berrill, Kenneth, 165n
Bhutan, 58
Biafra, 172n
bilateral aid, 63
Booker, H. S., 172n
borrowing, commercial, 45, 48
Brandt Report, 41, 54, 61, 71, 78–9

Brasilia, 51
Brazil: external debts, 167n; growth, 39; Negroes
  in, 81; oil imports, 59; rubber seed from, 24
British West Africa: colonialism, 90–105;
  immigration, 128–39; trade, 1, 2; see also West
  Africa and the individual countries
brotherhood, 40
Bududira, Bernard, 86, 89
Burma: ethnic groups in, 27, 28; public security,
  29
Burundi, 86; foreign aid, 51
Byres, T. J., 178n

Cairncross, Sir Alec, 44
Camara, Helder, 79
Canada, 58
capital: export, 27; inflow, 8; for infrastructure, 1;
  labour as substitute for, 11
capital formation: agriculture, 3; group variation,
  7; investment and, 44; statistics, 10
capital-intensive industries, 118–19
Cary, Joyce, 91, 171n
cash crops, 2–4, 5, 14, 26, 91
Catholic Church, and economic inequalities, 73–89
central planning, 18, 19–37
Ceylon, see Sri Lanka
Chaucer, Geoffrey, 73
Chenery, Hollis B., 38
Chile, external debts, 167n
China, 25, 27; central planning, 158; workers in
  Malaysia from, 3, 6, 7, 24, 26
choice: economic development and range of, 22;
  freedom of, 25–6, 31
Church, and economic inequalities, 73–89
churchmen, 35
civil servants, 35–6, 95, 146, 147
Clark Leith, J., 170n
cocoa, 2, 5, 24–5, 33, 92, 96, 98–103
Cocoa Buying Agreement (1937), 96–7
coercion, 23, 25–6, 31
coffee, 22, 33, 92
Cohen, Sir Andrew, 94, 99
collectivization, 49, 52, 83
Colombia, growth, 39
colonialism, 58, 75, 90–105, 171–2nn
commodities, stabilization schemes, 14–15
commodity agreements, foreign aid as, 60–1, 168
communication systems, 4, 32

180